25⁰⁰

RCH

D1609424

The Mapping of the Entradas into the Greater Southwest

THE MAPPING
OF THE ENTRADAS
INTO THE GREATER
SOUTHWEST

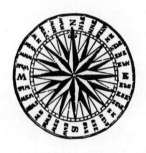

Edited by
Dennis Reinhartz
and
Gerald D. Saxon

UNIVERSITY OF OKLAHOMA PRESS : NORMAN

The book is published with the generous assistance of
Jenkins and Virginia Garrett.

Library of Congress Cataloging-in-Publication Data

The mapping of the Entradas into the greater Southwest / edited by
Dennis Reinhartz and Gerald D. Saxon.
p.   cm.
Includes bibliographical references and index.
ISBN 0-8061-3047-4 (alk. paper)
1. Cartography—Spain—History.   2. Southwest, New—Discovery
and exploration—Spanish.   I. Reinhartz, Dennis.
II. Saxon, Gerald D.
GA203.M36   1998
912.76—dc21   98-26958
                                                 CIP

Text design by Alicia Hembekides. Text typeface is Sabon.

The paper in this book meets the guidelines for permanence and
durability of the Committee on Production Guidelines for Book
Longevity of the Council on Library Resources, Inc. ∞

Copyright © 1998 by the University of Oklahoma Press, Norman,
Publishing Division of the University. All rights reserved.
Manufactured in the U.S.A.

1   2   3   4   5   6   7   8   9   10

To Brian Harley

Do not try to see an incredible world through a crack in the door, or by the light of a lantern search the teachings of maps and libraries. How would you believe that a line drawn on paper is the route of the sun . . . ? Fools, who are always seeking their own misfortune and bringing only trouble to kings!

The king of Portugal rejecting Columbus

CONTENTS

PREFACE

In the history of the Old World encounter with the North American Greater Southwest, few explorations were more enlightening than the three great entradas of Pánfilo de Narváez and Alvar Núñez Cabeza de Vaca in 1527–37, Fray Marcos de Niza and Francisco Vázquez de Coronado in 1539–42, and Hernando de Soto and Luis de Moscoso in 1539–43. The formative cartographic representations of this region of the New World that resulted from these expeditions were both fascinating and important, not merely for their geographic information and misconceptions, but also because of their influence on later exploration and discovery. One of the major ways in which these observations were broadly disseminated in the Old World, among a largely illiterate populace—at the time and for centuries thereafter— was via the manuscript and printed cartography of the period.

On February 20, 1992, The University of Texas at Arlington (UTA) hosted a symposium entitled "*Entrada*: The First Century of Mapping the Greater Southwest." It brought together five leading scholars in history, geography, and cartography to discuss aspects of the impact of early Spanish exploration on the Greater Southwest. The symposium also marked the opening of a major interpretive bilingual exhibition of many of the maps and related documents cited by the presenters. The exhibition was mounted on the sixth floor of UTA's Central Library. Both the symposium and the exhibit were sponsored and funded by UTA's new Center for Greater South-western Studies and the History of Cartography, the Libraries' Special

Collections Division, the Texas Committee for the Humanities, the Summerlee Foundation, the Association of American Geographers, the Friends of the UTA Libraries, and Jenkins and Virginia Garrett.

While the symposium papers reproduced in this volume address topics that span several centuries, they all relate closely to the creation of the cartographic images of the Greater Southwest based on the information from the first Spanish entradas into the region in the sixteenth century. By way of introduction, the state of Old World geographic and cartographic knowledge in the sixteenth century is delineated in "The Renaissance Geographic and Cartographic Background to the First Century of Greater Southwest Discovery and Cartography" by David Woodward, professor of geography at the University of Wisconsin at Madison and coeditor of the multivolume *History of Cartography* (1987–). Woodward also relates how Old World notions affected the depiction of New World geography and, in turn, gradually would be changed by it.

An early specific example of this change is discussed by David Buisseret in his essay, "Meso-American and Spanish Cartography: An Unusual Example of Syncretic Development." Using several striking examples from various collections, Buisseret, former director of the Hermon Dunlap Smith Center for the History of Cartography at the Newberry Library in Chicago and currently holder of the Jenkins and Virginia Garrett Endowed Chair in Greater Southwestern Studies and the History of Cartography at UTA, examines the fusion that occurred when Spanish and Amerindian cartographic styles came into contact. Buisseret concludes that both styles changed as a result of this contact, but eventually the European style gained the upper hand.

Harry Kelsey, currently Mead Fellow at the Huntington Library in San Marino, California, and author of numerous works on the Spanish borderlands, concentrates in "Spanish Entrada Cartography" on the sixteenth-century cartography most closely associated with the overland entradas. Robert S. Weddle, an independent scholar from Bonham, Texas, and the author of several important books on the Greater Southwest, including a trilogy on the history of the Caribbean Sea and the Gulf of Mexico, in "Coastal Exploration and

Mapping: A Concomitant of the Entradas" takes up the naval facets of the entradas and the resulting related coastal and other marine cartography. Kelsey's and Weddle's essays are complementary and together offer a rather complete examination of the maps resulting from both the entradas and the coastal explorations.

"*Legado*: The Information of the Entradas Portrayed through the Early Nineteenth Century" by Dennis Reinhartz, professor of history at UTA and a fellow of its Center for Greater Southwestern Studies and the History of Cartography, traces the legacy of entrada information and misinformation to be found on European printed maps from 1600 to 1802. All but one of the maps examined by Reinhartz are drawn from the superb map collections of Virginia Garrett and the Cartographic History Library at UTA.

The late J. B. Harley, professor of geography at the University of Wisconsin at Milwaukee, internationally renowned historian of cartography, and coeditor of *The History of Cartography*, was to have presented the concluding paper, but he unexpectedly passed away two months prior to the symposium. Brian was a good friend and colleague-mentor to many in the field of the history of cartography. He will be deeply missed. The symposium was dedicated to him, and so too is this volume.

The extensive exhibition that accompanied the symposium was mounted by Katherine R. Goodwin, cartographic archivist and exhibits curator for the UTA Libraries' Special Collections Division and author of numerous published works on the history and cartography of the Greater Southwest. She also helped to organize the symposium. To complete this volume, she has contributed a catalog of the items in the exhibit and a cartobibliography of the maps cited in the presentations and related to the entradas.

The essays in this volume focus on the entradas and the information revealed by them on the maps that followed. How this information defined the graphic images of the New World and, in turn, reshaped and broadened the horizons of the Old World is also considered. In addition, the linkages between the early Spanish explorers in the Greater Southwest, their influence on the indigenous peoples and vice versa, and the perceptions of this seductive region reflected on the first printed maps of the period are explored.

This volume is the third such Special Collections Publication of The University of Texas at Arlington. The first, *The Mapping of the American Southwest*, edited by Dennis Reinhartz and Charles C. Colley, appeared in 1987. The second, *The Mexican-American War of 1846–1848: A Bibliography of the Holdings of the Libraries, The University of Texas at Arlington*, prepared by Jenkins Garrett and edited by Katherine R. Goodwin, was published in 1995. As with the first two publications, proceeds from this volume will go to expanding the Special Collections Endowment for the stimulation and support of future publication activities of the Special Collections Division.

DENNIS REINHARTZ
GERALD D. SAXON

THE MAPPING OF THE ENTRADAS INTO THE GREATER SOUTHWEST

I. The Renaissance Geographic and Cartographic Background to the First Century of Greater Southwest Discovery and Cartography

David Woodward

On September 6, 1522, a Spanish *nao*, the *Victoria*, leaking from every seam, returned to the Guadalquivir River with a crew of 18, all that remained of Ferdinand Magellan's original expedition of five ships and some 270 men. The first circumnavigation of the world by a ship had been accomplished. It is sometimes forgotten, however, that the first *person* to circumnavigate the world was—in all probability—Henrique de Malaca, Magellan's servant-slave, who was acquired in Malacca but may originally have been from the Philippines or the Moluccas. Henrique may thus have completed his circumnavigation when he reached the Philippines with Magellan in 1521.[1] This possibility reminds us that the great age of European geographic exploration was never a one-sided endeavor; it always involved an encounter between explorer and the already resident population. Too often the story had been told only in European terms, as the progressive scientific filling in of geographic detail based on ever more precise European navigation instruments and techniques. As Brian Harley and others have stressed, however, the American Indian traditions of cartography already had their own independent cradle.[2] This was particularly true for Central America, confirmed not only by eyewitness reports, as when Hernán Cortés was given a "cloth with all the coasts painted on it," but also by other incidents. Later, Cortés wrote, "According to the map which the people of Tabasco and Xicalango gave me, I was to proceed from the province of Cupilcon to another called Zagotan." Or again, in 1540 along the Colorado River, Hernando de Alarcón

asked an elderly Indian to "set . . . down in a chart as much as he
knew concerning that river."[3]

It is difficult to imagine what some of the early European maps
of America would have looked like without the knowledge imparted
by the indigenous people. These sources, beginning with Juan de la
Cosa's world map of 1500, were usually unacknowledged and thus
constitute a hidden stratum in European cartography. It is also difficult to imagine the richness of the indigenous tradition that was
systematically and tragically destroyed by the Conquest, to the extent
that it may now be impossible to understand the silenced cartographic history of these indigenous cultures.[4]

This view rather dampens our celebratory fascination with the
technology of Renaissance exploration cartography. But there is
another point. The technology of navigation and cartography in the
age of exploration was no match for the theories that preceded it.
There has been a tendency for technical determinism in the history of
cartography, which has assumed that if a technological improvement
was made, it was immediately and universally applied. This has been
particularly true of the Renaissance, which is usually viewed as a
period of great innovation, and the deterministic cycle is repeated. I
hope to show that—far from effecting a sudden change—the Grand
Cartographic Theory of the Renaissance (in all its facets) took centuries to be converted into practice. With the benefit of hindsight, we
can see that this theory was ultimately to spell the hegemony of European mapping techniques throughout the world. But the apparent
precision of the early-sixteenth-century planispheres may be misleading. What did the maps mean, and how were they really used?

After the first circumnavigation, the immensity of the ocean—the
Mar del Sur—between America and Asia was recognized by
Europeans for the first time (despite the fact that Pacific Islanders had
long known this). The West Indies could no longer be confused with
the East Indies on world maps with any pretention to accuracy, and
the Americans had to be represented as a separate entity except by
those whose commercial minds were still rooted in the idea that
Cathay was simply part of the American mainland. Despite the

discovery of a large new continent between Europe and Asia, the search for a western passage through it remained a prime objective of European navigators throughout the sixteenth century and well beyond. A series of maps that Arthur H. Robinson has recently compiled dramatically illustrates the broad geographic questions posed in the early sixteenth century (plates 1.1–1.4).[5]

But in addition to being a barrier to the western route to the Indies, it also became abundantly clear from the European conquests of Mexico (1519–21) and Peru (1531–33) that the New World, as it came to be called by Europeans, was a prime area for settlement in its own right. The outline of the Gulf of Mexico began to take shape on maps.[6] Florida had been discovered by Juan Ponce de León in 1513 and the Yucatán in 1518–19 by Hernán Cortés, and both were first represented as islands (plate 1.5). Cortes's map of the Gulf of Mexico accompanied his second published letter (Nuremberg, 1524), which said that he was given a drawing of the coast by Moctezuma. The northern coastline, with its Spanish names, may have come from

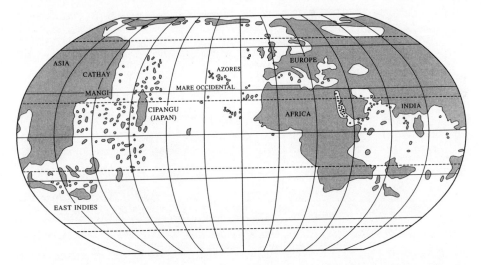

Plate 1.1. First of a sequence of four conversions of key world representations to the Robinson projection. The Martin Behaim globe (1492) produced before the Columbian voyages, severely underestimated the distance from Europe to Cathay and ignored the Americas and the Pacific. By permission of Arthur H. Robinson.

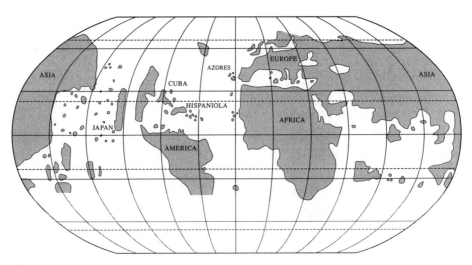

Plate 1.2. Line drawing of Martin Waldseemüller's world map on a cordi-form projection (1507) converted to a Robinson projection. Waldseemüller names South America "America" and postulated a small separate North American continent, but the Pacific Ocean is still basically ignored. By permission of Arthur H. Robinson.

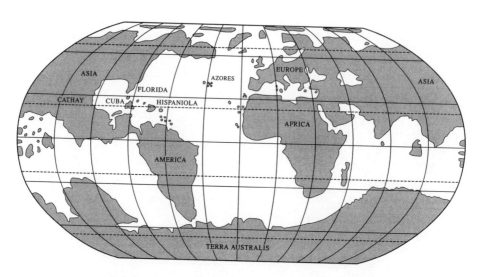

Plate 1.3. Line drawing of Oronce Finé's double cordiform world map, 1531, converted to a Robinson projection. It shows the commonly accepted concept of North America joined to the Asia continent and the width of the southern Pacific Ocean (following Magellan's voyage) as approximately correct. By permission of Arthur H. Robinson.

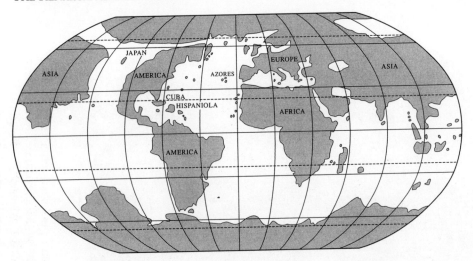

Plate 1.4. Line drawing of Mercator's double cordiform world map, 1538, converted to a Robinson projection. Mercator named both North and South America, but the width of the northern Pacific is still severely underestimated. By permission of Arthur H. Robinson.

members of Alonso Álvarez de Pineda's 1519 expedition, which had determined conclusively in an eight- or nine-month voyage that the coast from Florida to Mexico was unbroken and that a passage to the Pacific did not exist. A map known as the "Pineda chart" of ca. 1520—attached to a royal authorization of 1521 granting Francisco de Garay the right to colonize the country between Florida and Mexico—was the earliest to show correctly the main outlines of the Gulf.[7]

Several remarkable expeditions sought to claim the lands west and north of the gulf. From Pánfilo de Narváez's expedition in 1528, only four men led by Alvar Núñez Cabeza de Vaca lived to bring the tale—eight years later—of seven rich cities to the north. Fray Marcos de Niza claimed to have seen one of these, Cíbola, in 1539, with others in the far distance. Spurred on by this report, Francisco Vázquez de Coronado led a massive expedition in 1540–42 in search of the Seven Cities of Cíbola and another fabled city called Quivira (in modern Kansas). He found only Indian villages, but the cities remained on maps. While Vásquez de Coronado explored the

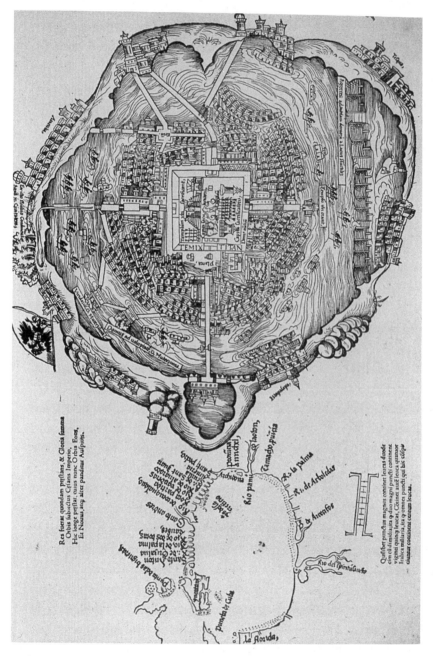

Plate 1.5. Cortés's map of the Gulf of Mexico accompanied his second published letter (Nuremberg, 1524) in which he said that he was given a drawing of the coast by Moctezuma. The northern coastline, with its Spanish names, may have come from members of Álvarez de Pineda's 1519 expedition. Photo courtesy of the Edward E. Ayer Collection, The Newberry Library, Chicago.

interior, Alarcón explored the Gulf of California and sailed up and down the Colorado River, and his pilot Domingo del Castillo drew a map in 1541 (now lost) which was subsequently published in the *Historia de Nueva Espagna* (Mexico, 1770). In 1539, Hernando de Soto led an expedition into the Mississippi valley, where he died of fever; the survivors, led by Luis de Moscoso, at length reached the gulf in 1543 with a report of their journeys. A sketch of the Soto expedition, ca. 1544, was found among the papers of the "royal cartographer" Alonso de Santa Cruz, in the Archivo General de Indias in Seville.[8]

This drama of exploration of the Greater Southwest in the sixteenth century was played out on a cartographic stage in terms of the Grand Cartographic Theory. What was this theory? Broadly speaking, it was the understanding of the fundamental need for a global system of measurement, an idea that has had a checkered history in the developement of mapping, even in the Enlightenment, and—one could say—also today. It was thus far broader than map drawing; it was a theory of geographic mapping, what Pierre Chaunu called "the great transition in dialogue between man and space."[9] It consisted of a number of assumptions: the sphericity of the earth, the value of measuring longitude and latitude astronomically, the structure of a systematic coordinate system, the breaking of the bounds of the medieval world from a three-part to a four-part world, the development of world projections, and the nature of a rhumb line in navigation. It tried to answer a series of often posed questions: how did pilots navigate when out of sight of land, how did they make maps of coasts thousands of miles from home, and how did they know where they were? Or, more specifically, what were the limits of precision in location? It raises the more general question of the difference between precision and accuracy and asks if it was possible in the Renaissance to have adequate accuracy of general coastlines without great precision in measurement and representation. In other words, did the rather low level of precision matter?

THE SPHERICAL EARTH

Basic to the Grand Cartographic Theory was the assumption that the world was round, a concept that has been understood by those who cared about the matter since the fifth century before Christ. It would not seem to be an issue for the period under consideration here were it not for the fact that, of the many myths associated with Columbus, none dies harder than the belief that he was responsible for this notion. Countless school texts and cartoons have perpetuated the idea. It derives from the famous story of Columbus's dispute with the scholars of the Talavera Commission at Salamanca around Christmas 1486 as told by Washington Irving, the most influential nineteenth-century biographer of Columbus.[10] The story of the rugged impetuous navigator arguing with the wise cosmographers has made him a folk hero: the triumph of common experience over scholarship in proving the world was round. But tracing back Irving's sources, there is nothing to suggest that this exchange had anything to do with the roundness of the earth. Indeed all the evidence points to common agreement on this question on both sides. Cosmographers seem to have been in short supply in Salamanca at the time, and Columbus got the dregs of the barrel. Their grasp of gravity was not perfect, but they knew the world was round. They said,

> If any man should sail straight away westward, as the Admiral proposed, he would not be able to return to Spain *because of* the roundness of the globe, looking upon it as most certain that whoever would go out of the hemisphere known to Ptolemy, *would go down*. And then it would be impossible to return, affirming it would be climbing a hill, which ships could not do with the stiffest gale.[11]

The origin of the notion of ships "falling off the edge" thus emerges. The theory of the earth's sphericity was of use to cartographers and navigators, but it must be said that this knowledge did not affect the life of the average medieval citizen one iota. There is certainly evidence from ballads—which presumably reached the unlettered classes more effectively than the scholarly treatises—that if the question of the shape of the earth was raised at all in the common mind, it was simpler to write it off as flat.[12]

THREE-PART WORLD TO FOUR-PART WORLD

The idea of the kingdom of God on earth drove the late medieval worldview: the transition from the three-part world to the four-part world constituted a spiritual crisis. The *mappaemundi* (world maps) of the Middle Ages represented the world divided among the three sons of Noah: Shem, the eldest, got the largest share, Asia; Ham and Japheth got Africa and Europe, respectively. The maps were allegorical, historical, and literary, a representation of the space of Christianity. The three-part earth is represented in the story of the three magi who visited the newborn Jesus. The Semitic, Hamitic, and Japhetic peoples derive from this powerful tradition. Often centered on Jerusalem, they were introverted to the interior of the classical and medieval world by a circumscribing ocean sea (plate 1.6). They were usually, but not always, oriented to the East, where the Garden of Eden was thought to be located. To the west, beyond the Pillars of Hercules, there was nothing: "Ne plus ultra" (Nothing more beyond). This self-imposed motto of the Old World was taken up as a challenge in the sixteenth century by Francis Bacon, who countered with "Plus ultra" (More beyond) in his "New Order" (plate 1.7). The possible addition of a fourth part of the world caused innumerable doctrinal problems far greater than whether the earth was round or flat. Since Noah had only three sons, from whom the entire population of the world had been descended, how could anyone inhabit a fourth continent, either in the antipodes or in Perioikoi, the Greek concept of a continent that was thought to be where America now is? Besides, no one could have possibly moved from the Old World to the New across the western ocean or across the equatorial torrid zone. First reports of peoples in a fourth part of the world were thus greeted with perplexity:

Plate 1.6. Section from a *mappemundi* by Ranulf Higden's Polychronicon showing the Pillars of Hercules. (British Library Royal MS. 14 c.ix ff. Lv–2.) By permission of the British Library, London.

North America comes to an end. From Mexico to Greenland Europeans have explored, described, and mapped the coast-line. Geographical misconceptions are still numerous; the outlines are frequently vague or faulty; a few major gaps in discovery, such as the Chesapeake Bay and Cabot Strait, still remain to be filled in later voyages; the names given to capes, Carolina, and a few Portuguese left stranded o Island by João Alvares Fagundes shortly aft coastal explorers of this period have not come t search out the land, which they have foun difficult, its natives hostile and primitive, and spices of their dreams unattained.

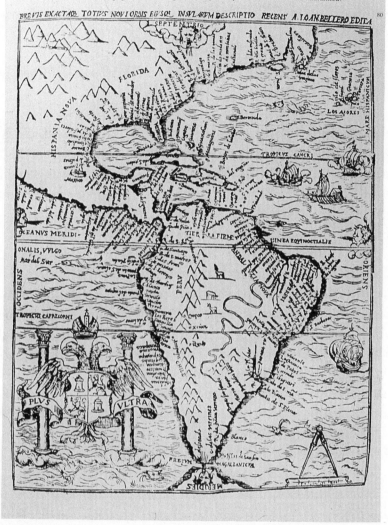

Plate 1.7. Woodcut map of the Americas by Jean Bellere, 1554. The "Ne plus ultra" (Nothing more beyond the Pillars of Hercules) of the ancients gave way to the "Plus ultra" of Renaissance exploration and the European discovery of "the fourth part of the world," on which the motto was proudly shown. In *Historia de México*, by Francisco López de Gómara (Antwerp, 1554). Courtesy of the John Carter Brown Library at Brown University, Providence, Rhode Island.

were they human and were they therefore under the Christian mandate to gather all the peoples of the earth into the fold? The antipodes were conveniently moved into southern Africa, pushed to the edges of the civilized world. The idea that there might be a fourth continent was conveniently forgotten.

PTOLEMY'S COORDINATES

The assumption of a spherical earth was obviously necessary for systems to describe positions on the globe. The core of this grand mapping theory came from Claudius Ptolemy, whose manual of mapmaking was the geographic bible of the Renaissance humanists. From the early fifteenth century onward, Ptolemy's coordinate system was quickly appropriated as an instrument of the first great age of European expansion into the overseas world. By reversing the introspection of the mappaemundi, the Ptolemaic world map projected an image of extroversion. The structure of parallels and meridians, with its numbered sequence of latitude and longitude values, explicitly recognized the other half of the world. Even if it was not a prediction of what was there, much less a measurement of what was known, it was a rhetorical visualization of the unknown, an invitation to fill the blank space and to explore that previously inauspicious West beyond the ocean sea.

The inauspicious West. There were nagging thoughts that there might be a way to the riches of the East across the western ocean. The idea had a pedigree dating back to Aristotle. Seneca, in the *Questions about Nature* (1.13), had stated that "the end of Spain and the beginning of India are not far distant but close, and it is evident that this sea is navigable in a few days with a fair wind." The Book of Esdras stated in its creation story that God "ordered the waters to collect in a seventh part of the earth; the other six parts he made into dry land" (2 Esd. 6). In the thirteenth-century *Opus Maius*, Roger Bacon recites this pedigree and illustrates the concept with a curious diagram (plate 1.8). Had this passage not been plagiarized almost

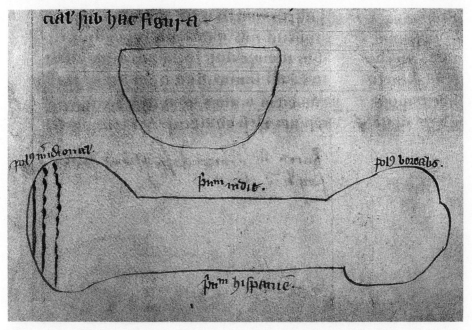

Plate 1.8. Roger Bacon's diagram of the spherical earth from an early manuscript of his "Opus Majus" (ca. 1275). It demonstrates his view of a short voyage between Europe and Asia and shows the two polar regions at either end of the narrow western ocean. (British Library Royal MS. 7 f.vii f.44.) By permission of the British Library, London.

word for word by Cardinal Pierre d'Ailly in the early fifteenth century, Columbus might never have been aware of Bacon's work: a copy of d'Ailly's *Imago Mundi* was one of Columbus's most heavily annotated books.[13]

Ptolemy's idea received wide exposure in the last quarter of the fifteenth century and was eagerly adopted by cosmographers, who tried to apply his concept to the mapping of the whole world. We do not know if Ptolemy could have foreseen what the historical effects of his invention would be, but the potential of a system of spatial reference as a source of power and inventory was quickly grasped in the Renaissance. So Jacopo d'Angelo, in presenting to Pope Alexander V the first Latin translation of Ptolemy's *Geographia*, wrote in the dedication that he hoped the book would serve as "an announcement of his coming rule . . . so that he may know what vast power over the

world he will soon achieve." As Samuel Edgerton put it, "the cartographic grid of the Renaissance was believed to exude moral power"; it
expressed "nothing less than the will of the Almighty to bring all human
beings to the worship of Christ under European cultural domination."[14]

It can thus be argued that the adoption of Ptolemy's projections
eventually made explicit the idea of the *whole-earth*. Ptolemy showed
180° of the inhabited world. Martellus extended it to 275°. In 1507
Martin Waldseemüller, in his *Universalis Cosmographia*, extended it
to 360°, again using Ptolemy's projection as the core, but he did not
extend it to the South Pole. The process was taken to its logical conclusion when Johannes Werner extended Ptolemy's projection in
1514 to cover the globe. No maps of the whole-earth survive from
the fifteenth century, but the interest in the concept of showing the
earth as a globe was obviously present. The references to globes
before Martin Behaim's globe of 1492 attest to it.

It is curious, therefore, that the rather modest map made ca.
1508 by Francesco Rosselli—graduated with 360° longitude and
180° latitude—is the earliest extant map of the world in the pure
(some might say "pedantic") sense of "map" and "world." It takes
on special significance as being the first contiguous map into which
every point on earth could theoretically be plotted and on which
every potential route for exploration could be shown (plate 1.9).[15]
Rosselli's oval world map is not only the earliest truly global map
that exists (globes obviously excepted).[16] It is the only such map to
survive between about 1508 and 1524, the date of a curious world
map by Juan Vespucci (plate 1.10). Here we have another crucially
important map that has received little attention. It is the first map of
the world to have been drawn after the circumnavigation of the
world: another picture of the earth from space, but one made after
the great hypothesis of the earth's sphericity had been proved.

Juan Vespucci, nephew and heir to Amerigo Vespucci, was an
examiner for the Casa de la Contratación. The purpose of his map
was apparently to make explicit the extension of the line of the
Treaty of Tordesillas on the other side of the world. The map is
annotated with a strange mixture of arrogance and humility: "Mira

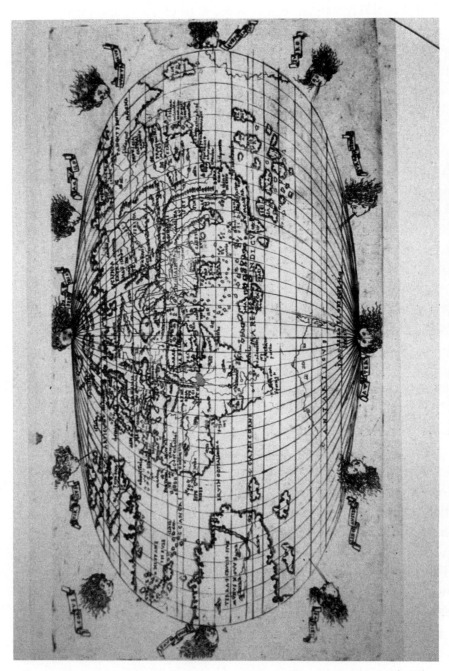

Plate 1.9. Copperplate world map by Francesco Rosselli, ca. 1508. It is the first contiguous map (as opposed to globe gores or globes) into which every point on earth could theoretically be plotted. Courtesy of the Arthur Holzheimer Collection, Highland Park, Illinois.

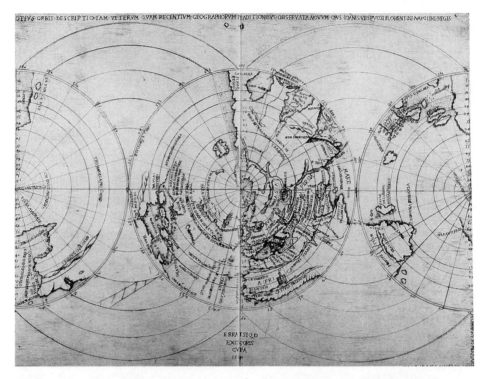

Plate 1.10. Juan Vespucci world map, 1524. The first extant map of the world to have been drawn after the circumnavigation of the world, Juan, nephew and heir of Amerigo Vespucci, drew it to make explicit the extension of the line of the Treaty of Tordesillas on the other side of the world. By permission of the Houghton Library, Harvard University, Boston.

arte et ingenio absolutum" (Wonderful art and perfect talent); "Errati si quod excusoris culpa" (As for the errors, may blame be excused). Its title is significant; it is neither a *tabula cosmographica* nor a *carta marina* but a *totius orbis descriptio*, perhaps the first map to bear such a title.[17]

The true meaning of "universality" was beginning to emerge in Renaissance cartography; it was a geographic idea of elegant simplicity. Robert Thorne could boast in 1527, "There is no sea unnavigable, no land unhabitable." The world could now be viewed as a carefully marked out stage on which the human drama could be played out. Atlases became theaters, as in the *Theatrum Orbis Terrarum* of

Abraham Ortelius's famous atlas of 1570 or John Speed's *Theater of the Empire of Great Britain*. Turn over their pages, and every map has a gridded backdrop on which the story of the Christianization of the world could be told. "The value of cartography had its most highly theoretical moment when plans of continents or of cities did more than describe reality, they defined it, and were capable of inventing and proposing the universe in the very act of reproducing it."[18]

PTOLEMY AND THE NAVIGATOR

But if the Ptolemaic coordinates had a crucial role in establishing the image and general position of America, they had very little immediate effect on the first century of practical navigation to the New World. The most obvious reason for this was that although latitudes could be fairly readily observed, longitudes were quite another matter. So there was little correct astronomical longitudinal data that could have been entered into a Ptolemaic grid. Thus, in the sixteenth century, two totally different kinds of maps were developed. The titles of maps reflect this ambivalence. A map compiled in the portolan chart tradition was called either a *carta da navigare* or a carta marina. It could be easily recognized by the superimposition of a compass rose and radiating lines. The other kind of world map, called a cosmographia or a tabula, was based on the Ptolemaic structure of longitude and latitude and plotted on various projections. The distinction between the two was explicitly recognized, and the maps often came in pairs. The classic examples are the two huge multisheet maps by Waldseemüller in 1507 and 1516, one of which was called "Universalis Cosmographia" and one "Carta Marina."

Portolan charts were a Mediterranean invention that seem to have emerged ex nihilo in the thirteenth century. They are technological marvels whose origins has still not been fully explained. They seem to have been based on books of sailing directions (statements of sailing distances with a traditional wind direction), and the earliest surviving example is the Carte Pisane (ca. 1275). The skewing of these charts of about 10° to 11° from true north seems to suggest that they were routinely based on the magnetic compass, although this instrument would not have been essential to their manufacture. Their frames result from the natural shape of the vellum, and their centers are arbitrary, based on the geometry of the radiating directional lines. Although confined to the Mediterranean and Black seas at the beginning, the scope of the genre was expanded to the known world (such as in the *Catalan Atlas*, ca. 1375).

As latitude sailing became more popular, portolan charts of the Mediterranean and the world planispheres began to be graduated in latitude in equal steps. Latitude could be simply measured by observing the height of the pole star above the horizon and applying a correction according to the position of the guards of the Little Bear. This was known as the Rule of the North Star and had to be memorized by the pilot in the form of a poem or mnemonic. During the day the meridian altitude of the sun could be observed with a mariner's astrolabe, but this calculation required tables showing the sun's declination (or angular distance north or south of the celestial equator) for noon on any given day. Rules were also established for how far on a given bearing the navigator would have to sail to change his latitude one degree. This was known as the Rule for Raising the Pole and was calculated for each quarter wind assuming a length of one degree at 17.5 Portuguese leagues (4 Italian miles = 1 league) at the equator. This figure was an intentional underestimation, as most navigators preferred to "have their reckoning before their ship" and so "to sight land after they sought it." Such calculations were also an approximate way of estimating longitude, although these figures were rarely shown on navigation charts.[19]

Navigation charts, when they included latitude, showed it as equally spaced from north to south as it is on the globe. These were called plain charts. Pilots began to complain that over a long ocean voyage the charts did not seem to be correctly predicting position, owing to the convergence of the meridians. In 1529 the Jewish scholar and professor of mathematics at the University of Coimbra,

Pedro Nuñez, became chief cosmographer and keeper of maps and instruments to the king of Portugal. In two fundamental texts on navigation, both published in 1537, he described the true mathematical nature of a great circle and line of constant compass bearing on the earth, the latter of which he found was a spiral.[20] This became known as the loxodrome, or a rhumb line when transferred to a map. Obviously, a map that could show rhumb lines as straight lines would be extremely useful. Gerardus Mercator provided just such a map in 1569 called "Nova et aucta orbis terrae descriptio ad usum navigantium emendate accommodata" (*for the use of navigation*); as he plotted latitudes farther and farther from the equator, he had to constantly enlarge the spacing of points to straighten out the rhumbs. It was mathematically impossible to maintain straight rhumb lines on the map and have equally spaced parallels of latitude, as the navigation charts before Mercator's had attempted to do.

Conversely, on some maps compiled on a grid of parallels and meridians, an attempt was made to superimpose the rhumbs related to the winds over the Ptolemic structure. The winds had been shown around the printed Ptolemaic maps of the fifteenth century and their manuscript versions before them, but the cartographers stopped short of drawing rhumb lines in their direction, no doubt realizing the mathematical inconsistency involved in such a procedure. The fashion seems to have been started by Benedetto Bordone in his *isolario* of 1528 with four winds diagrammatically shown on an oval projection, and the inconsistency reaches full-blown proportions in the so-called Sebastian Cabot map of 1544.

Mercator's 1569 world chart symbolizes the union of the two traditions of world maps in the sixteenth century. A "cosmography" could now also be a navigation chart. Longitude and latitude as well as straight compass courses could be shown. But it seems to have been a point of pride among sailors to use the "plain chart" rather than the scholars' "cosmographies" even though their rhumbs were hopelessly wrong. But more surprising, even after Nuñez had discovered the true mathematical nature of rhumb lines and Mercator had straightened them on a world chart, plain charts continued to be favored well into the seventeenth century.

The errors resulting from incorrect plotting of compass courses were also compounded, of course, by the assumption that the magnetic compass always pointed in the same direction. Some attempts were made to demonstrate where north really was on these charts by placing a graduated oblique meridian in the northern Atlantic where the magnetic variation was particularly worrisome. Fifteenth-century navigators knew of the existence of magnetic variation; Columbus noted it on his first voyage; many were ignorant of it; some denied its existence; others were terrified by its possible occult powers.

The presence of sound theoretical ideas for the construction of instruments, in addition, was no guarantee of their use by unschooled sailors. In 1508 Queen Joanna of Castile, citing practical problems in navigation, wrote to Amerigo Vespucci, then pilot major, that all pilots should be instructed in the use of quadrant and astrolabe. The Casa de la Contratación was founded in part for this purpose. But it is misleading to denigrate the quality of Spanish and Portuguese navigational techniques during the sixteenth century, for they proved equal to the task at hand. It has been pointed out, for example, that these methods were partly responsible for the early supremacy of Spain and Portugal in exploration and provided models that were emulated by other countries during the sixteenth century.[21]

THE USE OF CHARTS IN NAVIGATION (MAP VERUS TEXT)

The ability of navigation charts of the time to replicate position is, however, still open to question. Discovery was only the first step of the explorer's task; he had to describe what was discovered, so that it could be recognized, and determine its position, so that his successors could find it. No charts could be more accurate than the available navigation methods and instruments, and dead reckoning was subject to severe cumulative error. There was thus probably far more reliance on verbal description of specific positons than cartographic. The marine chart was almost unknown in northern Europe before the sixteenth century. Spain, Portugal, and Italy were using them routinely, as the well-known experience of the Casa de la Contratación in cumulatively plotting new positions on the *padrón general*, or master chart, suggests. In England or the Netherlands navigation depended on written books of sailing directions, or rutters. This changed during the sixteenth century. By 1574 William Bourne, author of the first English navigation manual, complained about "auncient masters of shippes" who "derided and mocked them that have occupied their cardes and plattes . . . saying: that they cared not for their sheepes skins" and thought they "could keep a better account upon a boord."[22]

For example, despite his uncontested brilliance as a mariner, there is a real question of the precision with which Columbus knew where he was, even beyond the general idea expressed by the famous adage "Before the voyage he didn't know where he was going, when he got there he didn't know where he was, and when he returned he didn't know where he had been." He was curiously unable to record correct latitudes, let alone longitudes. His main method of navigation was by dead reckoning with the use of compass, hourglass, and line, and the extent and efficacy of his use of the quadrant to find latitude has been brought into question.[23]

It is true that Columbus intended to make a map, as the prologue of the *Diario* tells us: he planned to compile a nautical chart of dead reckoning, provided with a network of rhumbs and scale of distances, and in addition to compose a book of latitudes and longitudes in the manner of Ptolemy. Neither has survived, if they were ever made, and it is significant that Columbus did not say he would compile a map on the basis of coordinates. He was a nautical type: longitude and latitude were for the cosmographers. So even had he produced the map he mentions so that others could replicate his position, it is unlikely that this would have been much help except in providing a general direction. Efforts to pinpoint his first landing site in the Caribbean that rely on the dead reckoning data provided in the journal are not only suspect in their historical and cultural significance, they are also subject to severe cumulative error when not verified with astro-nomical measurements.

It may be objected at this point that if charts were such an imprecise record of navigational position throughout most of the sixteenth century, how do the coastlines on these charts—for example, of the Gulf of Mexico or the Mediterranean—appear so similar to their modern outlines? The answer may lie in the comparative accuracy afforded by coastlines that are enclosed basins rather facing the open sea. It is easier to closely approximate the shape of a large continent, for example, with only a few astronomically observed points. Thus representations may appear accurate on maps when the coastlines are not particularly precisely known with many observations. Charts of water bodies such as the Mediterranean are made up of a series of contained smaller seas, in which the navigation measurements tend to be self-correcting, such as in the case of a closed traverse on land. Cumulative measurements can provide constant cross-checks, and the rigidity of the structure is thus assured. The same is true to a lesser extent for the Gulf of Mexico. Where coastlines are "floating," however, such as the east coast of North America, gross longitudinal errors and the lack of cross-checking provide for a less rigid structure. It is noticeable, for example, that the accuracy of the Mediterranean portolan charts fell off dramatically when the charting extended outside the basin.

The Role of Commercial Atlases

If the manuscript navigation charts, based on primary information, were imprecise, the derivative maps for the commercial market were even more misleading, representing rather a window on the commercial and cultural concerns of the day and providing a glimpse of the most general concepts of worldview and geographic location. The editions of Ptolemy's *Geographia*, approximately fifty between 1475 and the nineteenth century, some replete with maps "based on the latest navigations," were obviously intended for the armchair cosmographer and merchant, not for the navigator. Columbus owned a copy of the 1490 Rome edition, but he apparently did not annotate it until after his return from the first voyage.

Nevertheless, the maps that most people saw in the sixteenth century came from the great independent map and book publishers of Germany, Italy, France, and the Netherlands. Based on improvements in exquisite copper engraving and printing, the Italian composite atlases of the mid-sixteenth century were intended as aide-mémoires and browsing narratives rather than navigational aids on land or sea. Even the late-sixteenth-century atlases of Ortelius and Mercator were primarily commercial products that responded to updating and correction primarily by their clients. Perhaps the derivative nature of such atlases should not concern us overmuch; in many cases the maps on which they were based have disappeared, leaving the atlases as the only witnesses. For example, the well-known manuscript atlases of Battista Agnese, which have enjoyed a remarkable survival rate owing to their elegant beauty and collecting value, and which are usually regarded as having been bought as gifts for rich merchants and nobles, often contain surprisingly current and original information. For example, on a 1542 chart of Agnese, California is named for the first time based on the discoveries of Francisco de Ulloa, and indications of high and low water levels in the Vermilion Sea (Gulf of California) are also noted for apparently the first time.[24]

CONCLUSION

The Grand Cartographic Theory of the Renaissance, which contained all the ingredients of a mapping system that was eventually to be adopted worldwide, failed to be put fully into practice in the sixteenth century. Although the principles of Ptolemy's coordinates had been accepted in scholarly cosmographies and plotted on world maps, many of which found their way into print, practical navigators steered an entirely different course, preferring the plain chart that recognized neither the convergence of the meridians nor correct compass directions. Even the theoretical methods of measuring latitude were often poorly carried out in practice. It was thus very unlikely that a correct landfall could be made after a long transoceanic voyage using a small-scale sailing chart such as we have seen illustrated here. No doubt more guesswork was the norm: one found the approximate latitude and then sailed along it until a recognizable stretch of coastline was seen. Textual descriptions and drawings of features and personnel who recognized stretches of coast from previous voyages were therefore probably as much help as sea charts during this period. The apparent precision of these charts should not therefore be taken to indicate pinpoint accuracy, and efforts to reconstruct historical voyages using them without supporting evidence are doomed from the start. Maps in the sixteenth century are indeed slippery witnesses even when their outlines seem to herald the astounding effort in Spanish geographic exploration in the sixteenth century.

In 1948 the physicist Fred Hoyle said, "Once a photograph of the Earth, taken from the outside, is available . . . a new idea as powerful as any in history will be let loose." In a sense, the Grand Cartographic Theory of the Renaissance was a similar global system in which Europe had received a glimpse of the total world that was crucial in its self-definition. John Donne, in a beautiful passage in which he sees himself in his lover's eyes, epitomizes the idea:

> And now good morrow to our waking souls,
> Which watch not one another out of fear;
> For love all love of other sights controls,
> And makes one little room an everywhere.
> Let sea-discoverers to new worlds have gone,
> Let maps to other, worlds on worlds have shown,

> Let us possess one world, each hath one, and is one.
> My face in thine eye, thine in mine appears,
> And true plain hearts do in the faces rest;
> Where can we find two better hemispheres
> Without sharp North, without declining West?[25]

Perhaps this was the unconscious driving force behind the theory: the realization that the world was the finite home of humankind. That the practice sometimes failed to live up to the Grand Cartographic Theory does not detract from its power in shaping the European cartographic and geographic view of the world in the sixteenth and seventeenth centuries.

NOTES

1. Donald W. Brand, "Geographic Exploration by the Spaniards," in *The Pacific Basin: A History of Its Geographical Exploration*, edited by Herman Ralph Friis (New York: American Geographical Society, 1967), 118.

2. J. B. Harley, *Maps and the Columbian Encounter* (Milwaukee: Golda Meir Library, 1990).

3. Ibid., 81.

4. J. B. Harley, "Silences and Secrecy: The Hidden Agenda of Cartography in Early Modern Europe," *Imago Mundi* 40 (1988): 57–76.

5. Arthur H. Robinson, "It Was the Mapmakers Who Really Discovered America," *Cartographica* 29, no. 2 (1992): 31–36.

6. Raleigh Ashlin Skelton, *Explorers' Maps: Chapters in the Cartographic Record of Geographical Discovery* (London: Routledge and Kegan Paul, 1958; reprint Spring Books, 1970).

7. William P. Cumming, R. A. Skelton, and D. B. Quinn, *The Discovery of North America* (New York: American Heritage Press, 1972), 68–69.

8. Ibid., 173.

9. Pierre Chaunu, *European Expansion in the Later Middle Ages*, translated by Katherine Bertram, in *Europe in the Middle Ages: Selected Studies*, edited by Richard Vaughan (Amsterdam: North-Holland, 1979), vii.

10. Washington Irving, *The Life and Voyages of Christopher Columbus*, edited by John Harmon McElroy (Boston: Twayne, 1981), 48–50.

11. Ferdinand Columbus, "The History of the Life and Actions of Adm. Christopher Columbus," in *A Collection of Voyages and Travels*, 4 vols. (London: Awnsham and John Churchill, 1704), 2:576. My italics.

12. David Woodward, "Medieval Mappaemundi," in *History of Cartography: Cartography in Prehistoric, Ancient, and Medieval Europe and the Mediterranean*, edited by J. B. Harley and David Woodward (Chicago: University of Chicago Press, 1987), 1:286–370.

13. David Woodward, "Roger Bacon's Terrestrial Coordinate System," *Annals of the Association of American Geographers* 80 (1990): 113–14.

14. Samuel Y. Edgerton, Jr., "From Mental Matrix to *Mappamundi* to Christain Empire: The Heritage of Ptolemaic Cartography in the Renaissance," in *Art and Cartography: Six Historical Essays*, edited by David Woodward (Chicago: University of Chicago Press, 1987), 12.

15. David Woodward, "Maps and the Rationalization of Geographic Space," in *Circa 1492: Art in the Age of Exploration* (New Haven: Yale University Press for the National Gallery of Art, 1991), 83–87.

16. David Woodward, "The Image of the Spherical Earth," *Perspecta: Yale Architectural Journal* 25 (1989): 2–15.

17. Kenneth Nebenzahl, *Atlas of Columbus and the Great Discoveries* (Chicago: Rand McNally, 1990), pl. 25.

18. Manuel de Solá-Morales, "The Culture of Description," *Perspecta: Yale Architectural Journal* 25 (1989): 16.

19. John Horace Parry, *The Discovery of the Sea* (New York: Dial Press, 1974), 149–70.

20. E. G. R. Taylor, *The Haven-finding Art: A History of Navigation from Odysseus to Captain Cook* (London: Hollis and Carter for the Institute of Navigation, 1971), 175.

21. Carla Rahn Phillips, *Six Galleons for the King of Spain: Imperial Defense in the Early Seventeenth Century* (Baltimore: Johns Hopkins University Press, 1986), 132.

22. Parry, *Discovery of the Sea*, 169.

23. Rolando A. Laguarda Trías, *El enigma de las latitudes de Colón* (Valladolid: Casa-Museo de Colón, 1974).

24. Cumming, Skelton, and Quinn, *Discovery of North America*, 131.

25. John Donne, "The Good Morrow," in *John Donne's Poems*, edited by Hugh I'Anson Faussett (New York: E. P. Dutton, 1958), 1.

II. MESO-AMERICAN AND SPANISH CARTOGRAPHY

An Unusual Example of Syncretic Development

David Buisseret

When the Spaniards arrived on the American mainland, in April 1519, they were astonished to find that the native inhabitants habitually drew detailed maps of large areas of territory. In fact, this was unusual for the Americas; although other indigenous groups, both to the north and to the south, had traditions of mapping, these were not nearly so developed as the techniques of Meso-America. The peoples of this region were capable of drawing maps on a variety of scales. Some of the most interesting ones reflected their ideas about the world and its origins, but I will be concerned here only with their topographic maps and city plans, which showed relatively small areas of land. After identifying the salient features of both indigenous and Spanish maps, I will demonstrate how over the centuries a syncretic form emerged, in which eventually the European styles gained the upper hand.

FIRST SPANISH IMPRESSIONS

A considerable number of Spanish descriptions of indigenous maps survive from the period of initial contact, mainly in the writings of Hernan Cortés, Bernal Díaz del Castillo, and Peter Martyr.[1] Díaz del Castillo described how, during the early exchanges with Moctezuma, the latter gave Cortés "a sisal cloth on which all the rivers and bays on the north coast from Panuco to Tabasco—about four hundred miles—were faithfully painted."[2] On several occasions he also remarked on the great skill of Moctezuma's "painters," who could produce on sisal cloth lifelike images of battles and other encounters.

The large map of the north coast is also described in the second letter of Cortés himself.[3] As he puts it,

> Likewise I asked Mutezema to tell me if there was on the coast any river or cove where the ships that came might enter and be safe. He replied that he did not know, but would have them make a map of all the coast for me with all its coves, and that I should send some Spaniards to see it, and he would give me guides to accompany them, and so it was done. On the following day they brought me a cloth with all the coast painted on it, and there appeared a river which ran to the sea, and according to the representation was wider than all the others.[4]

Cortés duly sent some of his men, who used the map in exploring this part of the coast. Similarly, in 1525, he relied heavily on a map drawn by the inhabitants of Tabasco and Xicalango during his expedition into Honduras.

CHARACTERISTICS OF INDIGENOUS MAPPING

Indigenous maps must have been very fragile, for they have not survived; indeed, no strictly typographic maps have been preserved from the period before the Spanish Conquest. But a reasonable number of such maps have survived from the decades immediately after the arrival of Cortés, and these allow us to identify precisely the characteristics of indigenous cartography.[5] The maps eventually found in abundance in the Valley of Mexico seem to derive from the Mixteca region, which borders the Pacific Ocean to the south-southeast of Mexico City;[6] this is the area from which seven substantial pre-Conquest manuscripts have survived, though none contains a topographic map in the narrow sense of the term.

One of the purest indigenous maps is the one known as "Cuauhtinchan No. 1," now preserved at the Bibliothèque Nationale in Paris (plate 2.1).[7] It shows part of the province of Puebla, with the River Atoyac running through it. Tlaxcala is at the upper left, marked by a pile of rocks crowned by a temple; two white-clad figures sit nearby. At the bottom center is Cholula, with its three great temples, and in the center is Cuauhtinchan itself, between two ranges of mountains. At the top right is the Pico de Orizaba, now in the state of Veracruz. The delineation of the mountains has been held by some commentators to show European influence, but this is not obvious.

The river is shown in characteristic style, marked in blue with tributaries entering from red springs. A great assembly of chiefs is taking place in the center, at Cuauhtinchan; from their appearance these are Chichimecs. Many tracks lead out from this assembly to various locations, marked by distinctive glyphs. Many of these locations have arrows sticking out of them, which is the sign for conquest (and is reminiscent of the European convention of crossed swords to mark a battle site). There is not indication of orientation or scale, but it is easy enough to see what is being shown in general geographic terms. We have here a history as well as a geography, for this map is a crucial accompaniment to the "Historia Tolteca-Chichimeca" and shows the establishment of the Chichimecs in their new territory.

There is no such historical element in the next map, from the Codex Kingsborough in the British Library (plate 2.2, page 91). Also known as the "Memorial de los Indios de Tepetlaoztoc," it probably shows the town itself as the glyph with the open mouth at the top left.[8] The range of hills at the right may be the Sierra Nevada, forming the eastern boundary of the Valley of Mexico. Among the hills are settlements, marked by distinctive glyphs and linked by a road, marked with footprints. Similar prints mark the road crossing the valley floor, and there are sections of a river, top left and bottom right, that are also shown with distinctive wavy lines and eddy marks. At the bottom center is another rocky area, with the threefold knots that are the sign for "stone" interspersed with place glyphs, one of which shows the rising sun. About the only evidence of European

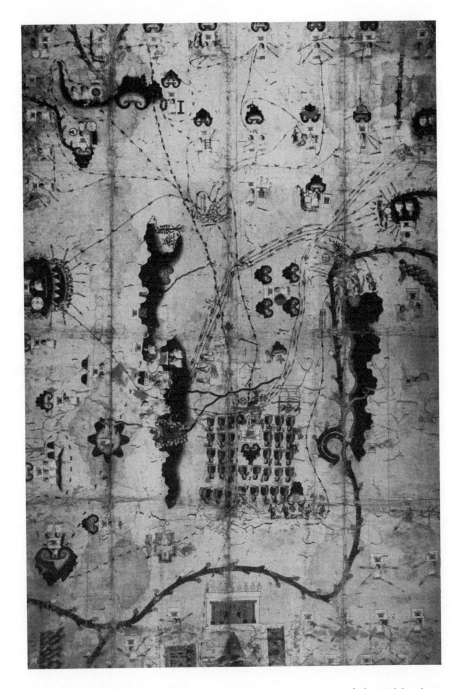

Plate 2.1. Map called "Cuauhtinchan No. 1." Courtesy of the Bibliothèque Nationale, Paris.

influence in this map is the delineation of the trees, which plentifully cover what may be the Sierra Nevada.

The Códice Xolotl brings us back to the earlier type of map, in which a story is interwoven with the geographic information.[9] Drawn in the early sixteenth century, it shows the Texcoco region, on the eastern shore of Lake Mexico. The codex has ten pages, the first of which we see here (plate 2.3). At the top left, Xolotl and his son Nopaltzin are visiting a Toltec family, identified by four blue circles, to collect tribute. This tribute may take the form of rabbits, turkeys, or, as at the top left, eagles. An eagle is shown immediately to the right of a mountain on which is a glyph consisting of an eye and a flag. As we work down this map, we find Xolotl and Nopaltzin visiting other families, sometimes with the standard blue circle identification, and passing alongside various rivers on the way. This map from the Códice Xolotl, with its highly simplified version of the land and its tributary peoples, represents the most elementary form of Meso-American mapping.

The "Mapa de Sigüenza" is another example of a combined map of time and space (plate 2.4).[10] It shows the voyage of the Aztec people from Aztlan (top right), which they left about A.D. 831, to Chapultepec, which they reached about 1142 (center left, mountain with grasshopper), and then on to Tenochtitlan by 1192; the latter city is shown surrounded by marshes. The figures emerging from Aztlan at the top right show a marked European influence, but the map offers good examples of characteristic Meso-American features: the road with its foot marks, the symbols to indicate towns, and the dots (probably) to indicate populations.

This traditional cartography could delineate towns as well as countrysides. The most famous surviving town plan is the "Plano en papel de Maguey," which is in fact drawn on amatl paper (plate 2.5).[11] This large panel (2.4 x 1.7 meters) shows part of a city, which most commentators agree is Tenochtitlan, or Mexico City. It seems to contain work from several different periods, the earliest of which sets out the rectangular blocks of the city about the time of the Conquest.[12]

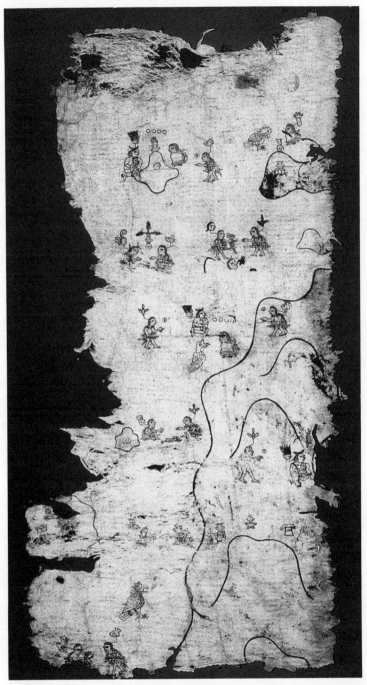

Plate 2.3. Map from the Códice Xolotl. Courtesy of the Bibliothèque Nationale, Paris.

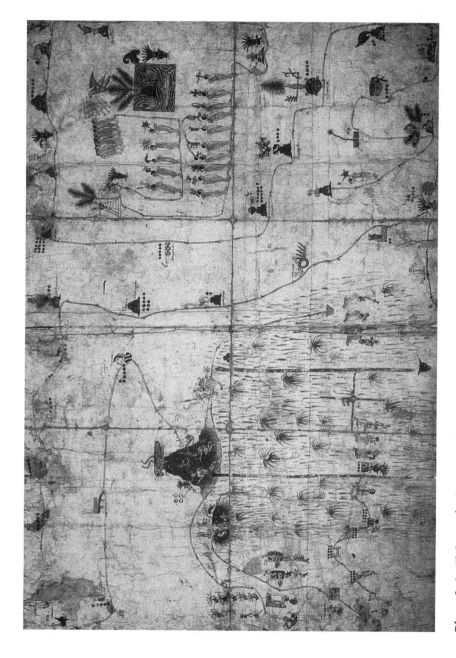

Plate 2.4. "Mapa de Sigüenza." Courtesy of the Biblioteca Nacional de Antropología e Historia, Mexico City.

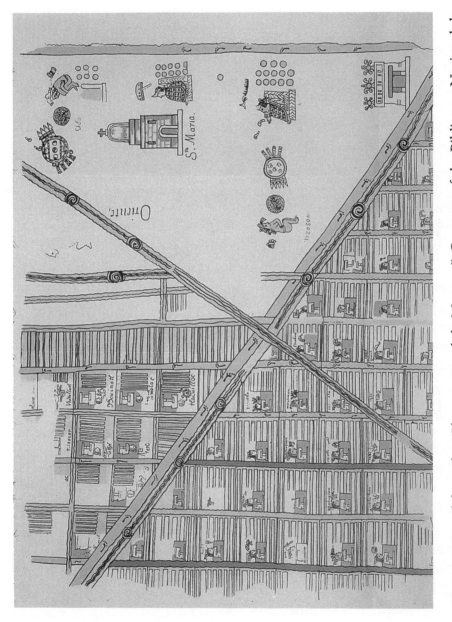

Plate 2.5. Detail from the "Plano en papel de Maguey." Courtesy of the Biblioteca Nacional de Antropología e Historia, Mexico City.

The city was then organized very coherently, and for each of the roughly square blocks there is a glyph identifying the householder. Canals and roads divide the city, with the major watercourses running on the diagonal. In the top right-hand corner of the detail are typical Aztec figures, joined now by the drawing of the church of Santa Maria. The "Plano en papel de Maguey" gives a powerful impression not only of the mapping skill of whoever drew it but also of the highly organized nature of the town plan; evidently the rectangular cities prescribed by the various sixteenth-century Spanish town planning laws had their Amerindian precursors.

CHARACTERISTICS OF SIXTEENTH-CENTURY SPANISH MAPS

Most of us will be familiar with the general nature of sixteenth-century Spanish maps, but it will be as well here to set out their general characteristics. Many of these may be identified on the remarkable map drawn in 1590 by the Spanish engineer Juan-Bautista Antonelli to show the road from the Gulf of Mexico, near Medellín, to Mexico City (plate 2.6).[13] The gulf is at the bottom of the map, which has both an orientation sign and a scale (both in the middle). Rivers and locations are identified in writing, and there is a long signed commentary at the side of the map. Conventional signs are used for forests and hills, and settlements are shown with small bird's-eye views; written descriptions further elucidate these, such as *ingenyo* (mill) or *estancia* (ranch).

The roads and rivers are indicated by coded colors, red and white for different kinds of roads and blue for the rivers. Note in particular the dense pattern of streams around and in Mexico City itself. When Antonelli wishes to indicate an unusual feature, he usually names it: hence the word *bolcan* by the drawing of Popocatepetl. This map is much more generalized than the Amerindian ones that we have been considering; no arcane knowledge is needed to interpret it, since the symbolism, in the shape of conventional signs, is relatively impoverished.

Plate 2.6. Juan-Bautista Antonelli, "Map of the Road from Medellín to Mexico City, 1590." By permission of the Ministerio de Educación y Cultura, Archivo General de Indias, Seville.

The same is true of the town plans produced by the Spanish engineers. Plate 2.7 (page 92) shows a plan of Havana, Cuba, probably drawn by Cristóbal de Rojas in 1603.[14] It has a scale, though no apparent orientation, and shows the outline of the city with planimetric precision, indicating the streets and the possible layout of the fortifications. A numbered key allows the reader to identify the main buildings. For the period, this is an exceptionally abstract plan, but it is characteristic of the way in which European town plans were developing at this time.

Alongside these more or less formal mapping traditions, there also existed in sixteenth-century Europe more or less informally drawn maps of the countryside. Their antecedents may probably be found in the landscapes drawn as backgrounds in the northern European paintings of the fifteenth century; be that as it may, such maps were becoming more and more common during the sixteenth century. Plate 2.8 shows one of these. Now at the Huntington Library, it delineates the English

Plate 2.8. Mid-sixteenth-century drawing showing the countryside in Buckinghamshire (England). By permission of The Huntington Library, San Marino, California.

countryside in the middle of the sixteenth century, with the aim of settling a quarrel between two adjacent villages. It is, in effect, a bird's-eye view, drawn with the maximum possible "naturalism"; in this respect, it is as far removed as possible from the highly abstract topographic maps of Meso-America.

THE PROCESS OF SYNCRETISM DURING THE SIXTEENTH CENTURY

Having identified the major features of the two traditions, we can now analyze the way in which the indigenous style was progressively invaded by European elements. One of the most spectacular examples of this invasion is the map of Mexico City attributed to Alonso de Santa Cruz, now preserved in the University Library at Uppsala, Sweden (plate 2.9).[15]

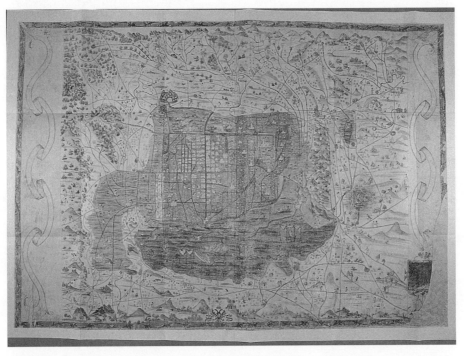

Plate 2.9. Alonso de Santa Cruz, "Map of Mexico City." Courtesy of the Uppsala University Library, Uppsala, Sweden.

This map was the product of the scriptorium at the Colegio de Santa Cruz of Tlatelolco, in Mexico City, where Franciscan Indianists studied the Indian world while Indian students learned "the essentials of fifteenth- and sixteenth-century European literary culture."[16] In its delineation of the city it no doubt relied on maps like the "Plano en papel de Maguey," but the actual way of showing the streets, the delineation of the surrounding topography, and the introduction of genre scenes to the countryside are all very European in style. Plate 2.10 shows a detail from the map including the very large representation of the Colegio de Santa Cruz in the middle left. Notice the Indians fishing in the lake in the middle right and the innumerable other figures throughout the countryside. Notice, too, the characteristically European scroll at the right, and the floral border, which seems to be an echo of the tradition of fifteenth-century northern European miniature painters. Santa Cruz used this map to generate one of the maps in his *Isolario general*, a much-simplified version of the plan called "Tenuxtitlan, Mexico," but otherwise his only connection with the plan is that it was found among his papers.

Another specialized map presumably dating from the middle of the sixteenth century is the one showing the mining district of Temascaltepec, now preserved at the Newberry Library in Chicago (plate 2.11, page 93).[17] Here the river is shown in the traditional fashion, but the roads are red, as in Spanish cartography. There are symbols for three churches, but also for five traditional house sites. The sites of the mines are shown by traditional glyphs, but the surrounding hills and forests are indicated in a European style. In short, the two traditions are fairly balanced in this map.

Many such maps exist in the Archivo General de la Nación in Mexico City, to which we shall return. But the greatest coherent body of topographic maps known for the sixteenth century is the series of *pinturas* (paintings), as they were called, that were drawn to accompany the *relaciones geográficas* (geographic reports) commissioned by Philip II of Spain; these are a mine of information about the process of syncretism. The king was a great collector of reports, and also an enthusiastic map user. From the late 1560s onward he had been

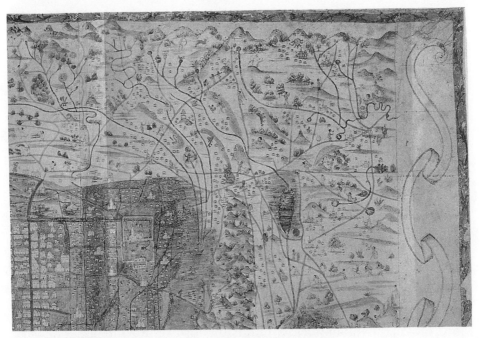

Plate 2.10. Detail from the Alonso de Santa Cruz map.

commissioning reports about his possessions on both sides of the Atlantic Ocean, and in 1577, under the direction of the *cronista-cosmógrafo* (chronicler-cosmographer) Juan López de Velasco, a particularly full set of reporting requirements was sent to the officials in the Indies.[18]

Among the fifty headings were two requesting maps:

> 10. Describe the site on which each town is established, whether it is on a height, or low-lying, or on a plain. Make a plan in color of the streets, plazas, and other significant features such as monasteries, as well as can be sketched easily on paper, indicating which part of the town faces north or south.
>
> 42. Note the ports and landings that occur near the coast, making a plan of each in color, as can be drawn on a sheet of paper, by which their form and shape can be seen.

In response to this request, many maps were drawn and sent back to Spain. They were at first lodged in the Archivo General de Simancas and then in the Archivo de Indias in Seville, but during the turbulent years of the late eighteenth and early nineteenth century some of them disappeared. At present the Archivo holds 27 of these pinturas, 12 are at the Real Academia de la Historia in Madrid, and 37 are at the University of Texas at Austin. I will examine seven of them, taken in alphabetical order, to assess the degree of syncretism present in each.

The map of Atengo, in the archbishopric of México, now preserved at Austin, has a yellow boundary running round its margin, and many glyphs as well as inscriptions (plate 2.12, page 94).[19] Along the top edge are seven mountain sign glyphs and one showing a spring (*ojo de agua*). Immediately below this row are two enclosure signs, meaning a ranch, and below them three more mountain glyphs. Sharing the center of the page is a Spanish church and the sign for the lord of Mizquiahuala; below him is the lord of Tezontepec. The very large hill at the left carries various glyphs and stands above the river delineated in typical Aztec style.

We do not know who produced this markedly Amerindian map. The *corregidor* (Spanish magistrate) for the *pueblo* (town) was Juan de Padilla, and he evidently relied on some local mapmaker. In the relación, the response to question 10 remarks that "the map [*pintura*] made of this area will answer the queries precisely and splendidly [*espléndidamente*]"; certainly it gives us a lively impression of Atengo and the surrounding villages.

The pintura and the relación of Cholula (plate 2.13, page 95) is apparently much more European in style.[20] It accompanied the report of the corregidor Gabriel de Rojas, and may have been drawn by him. Cholula was a great urban center in pre-Conquest Mexico, as is indicated by the Nahuatl title "Tollan-Cholula" below the glyph at top right. A Meso-American river runs just to the left of this glyph, but otherwise the map is European in its superficial appearance.

Closer examination reveals some surprising survivals. Six large churches are shown: Santiago, San Miguel, San Juan, San Andrés,

San Pablo, and Santa Maria. These are drawn in the European way, but after the name of each in the descriptive title comes the name *cabacera*; thus, "San Pablo, cabacera." This may be a play on the word *cabacera*, meaning either a head unit or a little hill. For in the background of each drawing of a church is also a little hill, or cabacera; evidently it was inconceivable to the person who named the churches that they could not be associated with a hill, as on the Aztec glyphs. Similarly, the texts written on the map contain many Nahuatl elements, such as *Angeles ohtli*, or road to San Angeles; *tianquizco*, or marketplace; *corregidor ichan*, or place where the corregidor lives. The ancient traditions are thus very much alive in this apparently Europeanized plan.

The relación for Mexicaltingo, in the archdiocese of Mexico, contains the pintura of Culhuacan, now preserved at Austin (plate 2.14, page 96).[21] The large church in the middle, top left, is according to the legend, "San Juan Evangelista, that is, Caulhuacan." Subsidiary churches dot the countryside, linked in most cases by Aztec-style roads; these bridge the rivers with a distinctive sign. In the center is an indigenous building sign and a mountain glyph; as the accompanying text explains, "because of this hill the place is named Culhuacan." Just to the right of the main church is the notation "this is the paper mill"; René Acuña believed that the map itself was drawn on paper from this mill. The pintura was the work of Pedro de San Agustín, but we have no means of knowing what his cartographic background was; certainly he held a delicate balance between the two traditions in his work.

For the adjacent province of Meztitlan, we have a pintura that is purely European in style (plate 2.15, page 97).[22] Here the *alcalde mayor* (mayor), Gabriel de Chávez, seems to have played a major role in drawing up the report, and may even have sketched the pintura. It much resembles contemporary bird's-eye views in Europe, such as plate 2.8, with its naïf but realistic view of the countryside. The town of Meztitlan is in the center, surrounded by the hills in which nestle its satellite settlements. There is some indication of cultivated fields down by the river, and here and there we see tracks linking the settlements. On the remoter hills, at the top of the pintura, we have a reminder that the Spanish occupation did not go unresisted; here figures of archers suggest banditry, or even guerrilla warfare.

In the diocese of Tlaxcala, about ten leagues south-southeast of Puebla, lay the town of Quautlatlaca (or Guautlatlaca). In the relaciones, it was linked with the adjacent settlement of Huehuetlan.[23] On the pintura, the church of "Santo Domingo Vevetla," or Santo Domingo Huehuetlan, is at the center left (plate 2.16, page 98). A network of red roads connects it with subsidiary parishes, which are named and in some cases have comments in Nahuatl. In the upper center of the right-hand page is a square enclosure; this is labeled "Yistancia francisco martiniz," the ranch of Francisco Martinez. The area colored brown and confined within a line is probably wooded rather than high ground. Either way, the terrain is shown in a manner consistent with the latest European techniques.

The pintura from the relación for Teozacoalco (plate 2.17, page 99) is without doubt the one that has received the most intensive study.[24] It comes from the Mixtec area, in the diocese of Antequera, and shows a remote region in what is now central Oaxaca. The map is drawn in a circular shape, following an ancient tradition, and contains many genealogical elements as well. These lists of rulers are so complete and accurate that they allowed Alfonso Caso to reconstruct the main elements of Mixtec dynastic history, by linking the dynasties of Tilantongo and Teozacoalco on the map; it was in effect the Rosetta stone for Mixtec codices.

The map is oriented with the east, or rising sun, at the top; from here various streams, drawn in the ancient way, coverage on the Río Verde, which will eventually reach the Pacific Ocean. A network of foot-marked roads covers the area, linking the center of Teozacoalco (center, left) with thirteen subsidiary settlements, each one marked by a small church. At Teozacoalco itself, there is a large church and also the plan of some dwellings, by which is written: "These are the houses of Don Felipe and Don Francisco his son, natural lords [*señores naturales*] of this place." The mountainous nature of the region is indicated by numerous ranges of hills, drawn in a way that seems to owe something to both cartographic traditions. They are, indeed, inextricably mixed in this marvelous map.

From the same area, about twenty leagues to the north and east, comes the pintura that accompanied the relación for Texúpa; it is now preserved in the Real Academia de la Historia in Madrid, and has been studied by Joyce Waddell Bailey (plate 2.18, page 100).[25] Oriented to the southeast, it gives a very good impression of the rectilinear city, traversed by roads and streams and hemmed in by the hills. The outline of the hills is characteristically indigenous (see also plate 2.12, page 94), and the two large ones at the top both bear native symbols: a corn tassel and a flower. Arrows are sticking into the left-hand hill, perhaps symbols of conquest. Below the right-hand hill is a Mixtec temple symbol; a house symbol may just be seen on the hill to the left.

In the lower half of the pintura is the Spanish church and square. The latter is fed by a stream and has European style trees sketched in its interior; plants in the same style also line the rivers, which convincingly emerge from the mountains. The report for Texúpa was drawn up by the corregidor Diego de Avendaño, but the pintura must be the work of somebody thoroughly familar with Mixteca carto-graphic forms.

The huge corpus of maps preserved at the Archivo General de la Nación in Mexico City basically follows the same stylistic patterns as those we have observed among the pinturas. Here and there we find European intrusions at an early period; plate 2.19 (page 101), for instance, shows a map of Ocotlan and Simitlan, in the Valley of Oaxaca, that was drawn in 1534 in an exceptionally unindigenous style.[26] The rivers and mountains and roads are shown by the author, Bernave Sarmiento de Vera, "escribano de su majestad" (His Majesty's scribe), in the European way. There are no glyphs, and all information about locality is conveyed in writing.

Plate 2.20 is more typical for the sixteenth century. Apparently drawn by Gaspar Covarrubias in 1579, it shows the lands of Juan de Azanda in a largely indigneous style.[27] The mountains and rivers derive from that tradition, as do the house signs; there is also a hill

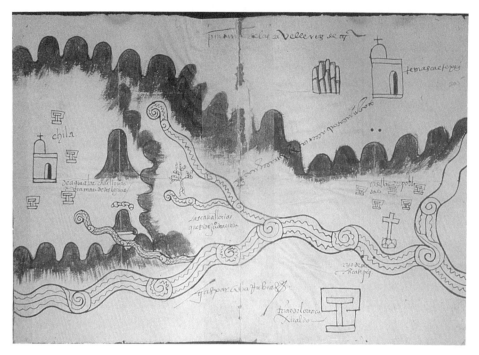

Plate 2.20. Gaspar Covarrubias, alcalde, "Map of the Lands of Juan de Azanda (Temascaltepec), 1579." Courtesy of the Archivo General de la Nación, Mexico City.

glyph at the center left. Spanish intrusions are confined to the symbols for the churches and the cross and to the way in which locations are named in writing. The Archivo General de la Nación is rich in maps of this kind from this period, some of which may have been destined for the relaciones geográficas, or at any rate inspired by the production of so many pinturas.

THE FADING OF THE INDIGENOUS TRADITION

As time went by, the maps produced in Mexico tended more and more to lose their indigenous features and to conform more and more to European traditions. Plate 2.21 (page 102) offers a good example of this tendency.[28] Drawn in 1589 by Gabriel de Chávez, it shows the road from Zenpoala (top right) to San Miguel (lower left). There is a church symbol at each of these locations, and the road is bordered by cactus-dotted hills. The oxcart and the pack mules are attended by drivers in European dress, and numerous written legends explain the road and sites. About the only remaining indigenous features are the rising sun, showing the *oriente* (east) at the top left, and the footprints on the broad brown road.

Of course, this tendency for the indigenous elements to become effaced did not proceed generally and in a uniform way. As late as 1599, for instance, the map of Coquila drawn by Alonso Morán was almost purely indigenous in style (plate 2.22).[29] The inscriptions and the church are the only elements recalling Europe; the roads, rivers, house sign, orientation marks, and leopard glyph all come from the ancient local tradition.

Two types of maps eventually replaced these early syncretic works. Plate 2.23 is representative of the first type.[30] Drawn in 1698 by some anonymous draftsman, it shows in the middle a block of land held at Yutzacono (Oaxaca). There are two European-style orientation marks, and the outline of the property is indicated by a line with letters along it; here and there trees, hills, and buildings help to give some idea of location. This rather naïf style is very typical of the local work produced in New Spain during the late seventeenth and eighteenth century; indeed, it rather resembles the better-known Californian *diseños* (sketches).

Alongside these rustic productions we also find maps drawn in the latest European style. An example of these would be the plan of the pueblo of Los Reyes compiled in 1783 by Francisco Antonio Guerrero y Torres, described as *agrimensor*, or land surveyor (plate 2.24).[31] There is a scale at the bottom left and an orientation symbol in the center. Each of the areas is lettered, no doubt to a main key, and the size of the sides of many of the fields is clearly shown. One road enters the settlement from the west (bottom of the map), and another cuts across its top portion. A river winds through the middle of the lands of the pueblo, whose houses and church appear to be plotted with some precision. This is a plan typical of those found

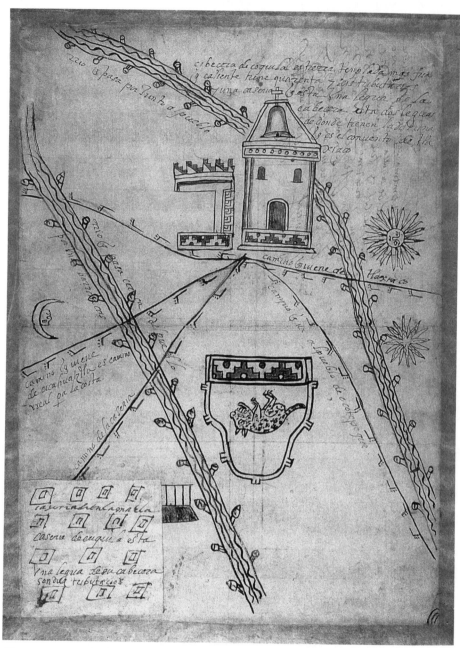

Plate 2.22. Alonso Morán, "Map of Coquila (Oaxaca), Mexico, 1599."
Courtesy of the Archivo General de la Nación, Mexico City.

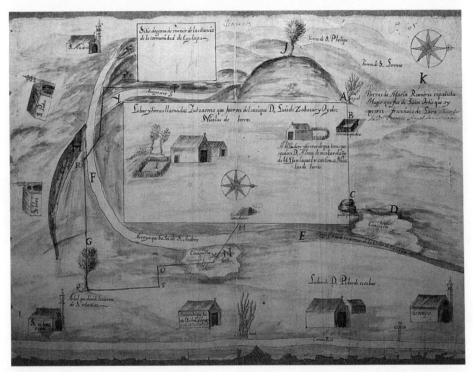

Plate 2.23. Anonymous, "Map of Yutzacono and Santa Maria Azompa (Oaxaca), 1698." Courtesy of the Archivo General de la Nación, Mexico City.

throughout western Europe during the eighteenth century, probably the great age for detailed land surveys of this kind.

CONCLUSION

We have come, then, from a time when the countryside of New Spain was shown according to indigenous traditions to one in which purely European styles predominates. The remarkable thing about this development is not that the native styles were effaced—after all, this was the period when European cartographic methods were conquering the whole world—but that they persisted for so long. In this

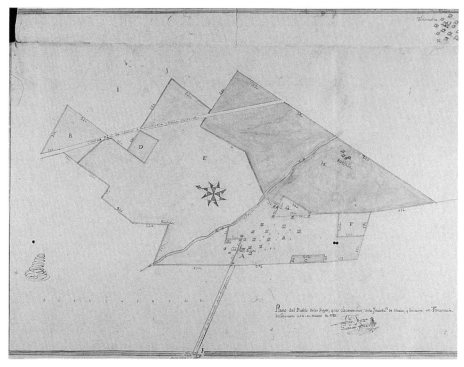

Plate 2.24. Francisco Antonio Guerrero y Torres, "Map of Los Reyes, 1783." Courtesy of the Archivo General de la Nación, Mexico City.

way, they gave rise for a time to a syncretic style of cartography, unique for the Americas and perhaps for the whole world.

In a wider context, this reflects the general durability of early Meso-American ways, which long continued to thrive—in some cases to the present day—in such other areas as dress, cuisine, and music. Such survivals seem more debatable in the areas of medicine, language, and law. George Kubler has written a good deal about the process of syncretism in art and architecture.[32] His observation that the Franciscan churches of New Mexico show greater evidence of Indian influence than those of California perhaps bears on the problem of why Meso-American mapping traditions were so durable. Where there survived a substantial Indian population, with deep-rooted traditions in some area of cultural activity, it was very likely that these traditions would for a time live on, giving rise to the remarkable syncretic forms that we have observed.

NOTES

I wish to acknowledge the help of John Aubrey and Bill Autry; they first introduced me to the bibliography of this subject, and have remained my indispensable guides. Of course, any errors or omissions are my own.

1. See for instance, Peter Martyr, *De orbe novo*, 2 vols. (New York/London: G. P. Putnam's Sons, 1912), 2:103.

2. Bernal Díaz del Castillo, *The Conquest of New Spain*, translated by J. M. Cohen (London: Penguin Books, 1986), 166.

3. Hernan Cortés, *Letters from Mexico*, edited by Anthony Pagden (New Haven: Yale University Press, 1986), 94.

4. Díaz del Castillo, *Conquest of New Spain*, 340.

5. The fullest general treatment of this theme is found in the contributions to the *Handbook of Middle American Indians*, 16 vols. edited by Robert Wauchope (Austin: University of Texas Press, 1964–1976): vol. 12, Howard F. Cline, "The *Relaciones Geográficas* of the Spanish Indies, 1577–1648," and Donald Robertson, "The Pinturas (Maps) of the Relaciones Geográficas, with a Catalog"; and vol. 14, John Glass, "A Survey of Native Middle American Pictorial Manuscripts." Substantial collections of facsimiles of Meso-American maps may be found in René Acuña, ed., *Relaciones geográficas del siglo XVI*, 10 vols. (Mexico City, 1982–1988); Duke of Alba, ed., *Mapas españoles de América siglos XV–XVIII* (Madrid, 1951); the *Catálogo de ilustraciones*, 14 vols. (Mexico City: Archivo General de la Nación, 1979–82); and *El territorio mexicano* (Mexico City: Universidad Autónoma de México, Instituto de Investigaciones Antropologías, 1982).

6. Mary Elizabeth Smith, *Picture Writing from Ancient Southern Mexico* (Norman: University of Oklahoma Press, 1973), 3.

7. It has been commented on by Bente Bittmann Simons, *Los mapas de Cuauhtinchan y la Historia Tolteca-Chichimeca* (Mexico City: Instituto Nacional de Antropología e Historia, 1968); Gordon Brotherston,

Image of the World (London: Thames and Hudson, 1979); John Glass, *Catálogo de la collección de codices* [in the Museo Nacional de Antropología, Mexico City] (Mexico City, 1964); Max Leinekugel la Coq, *Premières images de la terre* (Paris, n.d.); and Jorge Tamayo, *Geografía general de Mexico* (Mexico City: Editorial Trillas, 1962).

8. See the commentaries by E. Guzmán, "The Art of Mapmaking among the Ancient Mexicans," *Imago Mundi* 3 (1939): Thames and Hudson, 1–6; P. D. A. Harvey, *The History of Topographical Maps* (London: Thames and Hudson, 1980); and Donald Robertson, *Mexican Manuscript Painting of the Early Colonial Period* (New Haven: Yale University Press, 1959).

9. For commentaries, see C. A. Burland, "The Map as a Vehicle of Mexican History," *Imago Mundi* 15 (1960): 11–18; Charles E. Dibble, *Códice Xolotl* (Mexico City: Universidad Nacional Autónoma de México, 1951); J. B. Harley, *Maps and the Columbian Encounter* (Milwaukee: Golda Meir Library, 1990); and Robertson, *Mexican Manuscript Painting*.

10. See commentaries by Glass, *Catálogo de la collección*, and Walter Mignolo, "Colonial Situations, Geographical Discourses and Territorial Representations," *Dispositio* 14 (1989): 93–140.

11. See Glass, *Catálogo de la collección*; Robertson, *Mexican Manuscript Painting*; and the atlas accompanying the edition of Bernal Díaz, *The True History*, by Alfred Percival Maudslay (London: Hakluyt Society, 1910). This atlas has a redrawing of the *plano*, which I have used here.

12. On the whole question of precontact urbanism, see George Kubler, *Mexican Architecture of the Sixteenth Century*, 2 vols. (New Haven: Yale University Press, 1948).

13. On this engineer, see Diego Angulo Iñiguez, *Bautista Antonelli: Las fortificaciones americanas del siglo XVI* (Madrid: Hauser y Menet, 1942); the map is reproduced by Alba, *Mapas españoles*.

14. On this engineer, see Eduardo de Mariátegui, *El Capitán Cristóbal de Rojas* (Madrid: Centro de Estudios y Experimentos de Obras Públicas, 1985).

15. This map is fully analyzed in S. Linné, *El Valle y la Ciudad de Mexico en 1550* (Stockholm, 1948).

16. Robertson, *Mexican Manuscript Painting*, 155.

17. In interpreting this map I have relied heavily on the excellent article of Nadine Beligand, "Des Terres en question," *Trace* 10 (1986): 74–85.

18. See Cline, "The *Relaciones Geográficas* of the Spanish Indies, 1577–1648."

19. Acuña, *Relaciones geográficas*, 6, 39; and J. B. Harley, "Rereading the Maps of the Columbian Encounter," *Annals of the Association of American Geographers* 82 (1992): 523–42.

20. This pintura is reproduced in Acuña, *Relaciones geográficas*, 5, 126, and in *El territorio mexicano*; see also the comments of Smith, *Picture Writing*, 70.

21. Reproduced by Acuña, *Relaciones geográficas*, 7, 30.

22. Reproduced by Acuña, *Relaciones geográficas*, 7, 70. See also the excellent commentary in Alexander M. Tait, "Cartography and Colonial Society: Maps of the *Relaciones Geográficas* of Mexico and Guatemala" (Master's thesis, Department of Geography, University of Wisconsin at Madison, 1991).

23. Acuña, *Relaciones geográficas*, 5, 197–216.

24. Ibid., 3, 133; Brotherston, *Image of the World*; and Alfonso Caso, "El Mapa de Teozacoalco," *Cuadernos Americanos* 47 (1949): 145–81.

25. See her article, "Map of Texúpa (Oaxaca, 1579): A Study of Form and Meaning," *Art Bulletin* 54 (1972): 452–72; and also Acuña, *Relaciones geográficas*, 3, 215.

26. See the *Catálogo de ilustraciones*, 6, 151.

27. Ibid., 4, 120.

28. Ibid., 5, 107. See also the remarkable plates in Gisela von Wobeser, *La formación de la hacienda en la época colonial* (Mexico City: Universidad Nacional Autónoma de México, Instituto de Investigaciones Historicas, 1983).

29. *Catálogo de ilustraciones*, 5, 142.

30. Ibid., 2, 50.

31. Ibid., 4, 164.

32. See particularly Thomas F. Reese, ed., *Studies in Ancient American and European Art: The Collected Essays of George Kubler* (New Haven: Yale University Press, 1985).

III. Spanish Entrada Cartography

Harry Kelsey

The last two decades of the fifteenth century opened a period of stunning geographic expansion for Europe. Traders from Portugal charted the long, daring, and highly profitable ocean route to Asia. Bristol fishermen edged farther across the western ocean, searching for new waters in which to drop their nets. Cristóbal Colón returned to Spain in 1493 and reported that he had reached Asia by sailing west. A year later the Cabots, John and Sebastian, were back in Bristol, claiming they had seen land on a voyage to the northwestern ocean fisheries. By the end of the century the Cabots had visited this western land again, while Colón and others had made additional voyages to the west.[1]

Were these western voyagers really in Asia? There was wide debate in Spain and elsewhere among cartographers, geographers, philosophers, and theologians, but little agreement on details. One thing was clear. The new lands lacked strong central rulers. The Spanish king moved in several ways to fill the void, chartering towns and trading companies, granting lands and governing authority to men who were bold and callous enough to seize their opportunities, and calling on his cosmographers to draw accurate maps of the locations and routes to his new domains.

As with most endeavors, the work started in some confusion, but it soon developed in a more organized way. Seville was chosen as the headquarters in 1503 for the Casa de Contratación which administered the business of the New World empire.[2] Juan de la Cosa is usually considered to have been the first official cosmographer, and his famous world map is said to be an outstanding example of the sort of cartography then practiced at the Casa. Among the other great mapmakers of Seville were Andrés de Morales, whose work was widely acclaimed by geographers and seafaring men, Juan Díaz de Solís, and Amerigo Vespucci.[3]

By 1508, when it became clear that the Casa needed a resident navigational expert, Amerigo Vespucci was named *piloto mayor* (pilot major) and authorized to examine and license pilots who wanted to navigate ships in the Indies. He was also directed to prepare an official set of maps, or *padrón general*, of the newly discovered lands. With the imposing name *padrón real*, or master chart, these were required equipment for all pilots navigating ships to the Indies.[4] Already a noted explorer and cartographer, Vespucci had been made even more famous by the geographic work of Martin Waldseemüller, and gained a fine reputation throughout Europe.[5] Gonzalo Fernández de Oviedo, appointed by the Spanish Crown to record events in the Indies, called him "a great man of the sea and a learned cosmographer."[6] So little of his cartographic work has survived that it is nearly impossible to rate it in comparison with that of other cartographers of the time.[7]

When Amerigo Vespucci died in 1512, Juan Díaz de Solís, also an experienced navigator, was named to take his place. Within a few months Juan Vespucci, nephew of the first piloto mayor, was appointed to assist Díaz de Solís in preparing a new padrón real on parchment. All pilots going to the Indies were required to use it, and Juan Vespucci alone was authorized to provide copies (plate 3.1).[8] Concerned largely with sea routes and seaports, the padrón real also included general information about regional geography, but this was not the main focus, and no organized effort was made to keep interior geography up to date. Nevertheless, the padrón is a good but mostly unused source of information about the entradas, the Spanish expeditions sent to occupy and colonize the frontiers of New Spain.

The new padrón was not redrawn immediately after the appointment of Díaz de Solís, and it is difficult to say exactly when

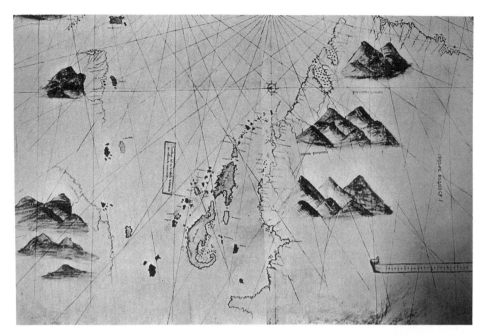

Plate 3.1. The "Pesaro Map" of about 1508 is generally said to be the work of Juan Vespucci (Computer-enhanced detail). Courtesy of the Biblioteca Oliverana de Pesaro, Pesaro, Italy.

representations of the present United States first appeared on Spanish maps. Some early maps such as the Juan de la Cosa map of 1500, the Cantino map of 1502, and the Waldseemüller maps of 1507 and 1513 seem to depict strange land masses near Cuba. Several historians have concluded that these depictions are evidence of early, unrecorded voyages to Florida. It seems more likely, however, that the places really represent Yucatán, the northern coast of North America, or the east coast of Asia.[9]

As for the padrón real, Díaz de Solís gave his official approval to the padrón of Andrés de Morales, perhaps because Díaz de Solís was still working on his own padrón general.[10] The Morales map of the New World may very well resemble the Egerton MS. 2803 in the manuscript collection of the British Library. According to Arthur Davies, who dates it at 1510, the map was "probably made from a copy issued by the authority of Amerigo Vespucci."[11] Whether this

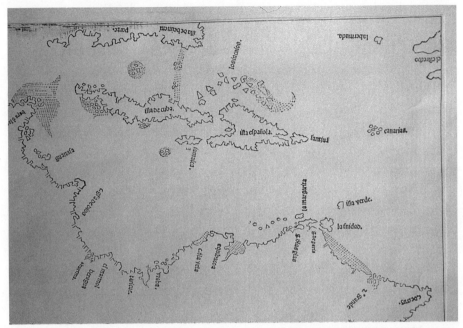

Plate 3.2. A map by Andrés de Morales, printed in 1511, shows the island of Bimini just north of Cuba. In *Opera. Legatio babilonica. Occeanea decas. Poemata*, by Peter Martyr (Hispali: Jacobum Corumberger Aleman, 1511). Photo courtesy of the Edward E. Ayer Collection, The Newberry Library, Chicago.

map was drawn by Morales or not, it is certain that Peter Martyr used the nautical map drawn by Morales in the 1511 edition of his letters. This printed copy of the Morales padrón shows the islands of the Caribbean, with a small portion of an island called Bimini lying just at its northern edge (plate 3.2).[12]

According to Fernández de Oviedo there was a story circulating among the Indians of the Caribbean that somewhere in the northwest lay an island called Bimini with a marvelous fountain, whose waters could turn old men into vigorous youths.[13] Martyr, the early chronicler of Spanish exploration, thought this was a most amusing story, but many at the Spanish court believed it,[14] and Ponce de León had no trouble gathering an expedition to find the place.

As it turned out, Juan Ponce de León did not discover the island of Bimini. He landed instead on the east coast of Florida, so named because he discovered it during Pascua Florida, the Easter season of 1513. He explored for six months, sailing around to the west side, and then turned back. Thinking he had perhaps discovered another island, Ponce de León secured a royal grant to colonize both Bimini and Florida but spent the next few years in Spain and on his estates in the island of San Juan (Puerto Rico).[15]

Then in 1519 Alonso Álvarez de Pineda sailed around the coast of the Gulf of Mexico and drew a map showing that Florida was part of the mainland (plate 3.3).[16] It was enough to convince Ponce de León that he should return to Florida, but this time the results were disastrous. The attempt at settlement failed. Ponce de León himself was wounded and later died.[17] His general route is shown on the map of Álvarez de Pineda, who credited Ponce de León with the discovery of "Florida which they called Bimini." According to this map Juan Ponce de León explored the coastline perhaps as far west as modern Pensacola ("Juan Ponce discovered up to here").[18]

Despite his tremendous respect for the man, Fernández de Oviedo thought it was very funny for Ponce de León to be chasing after "that fabulous fountain of youth that the Indians claimed made old men into boys." He added dryly, "I have seen it (but without the fountain), not in the restoration of vigor, but in the weakening of the mind; men become childish and lose their senses. Juan Ponce was one of them. How stupid to believe the Indians in such nonsense."[19]

Even with the testimony of Álvarez de Pineda, there was considerable reluctance to believe that Florida was not an island. The world map in Turin (ca. 1520–25), often said to be the work of Juan Vespucci, shows it this way.[20] Another map of the gulf, also apparently Spanish, equivocates, with several possible straits or rivers separating the peninsula from the rest of the mainland. This is the map published in the Latin edition of the Second Letter of Hernán Cortés.[21] It bears only a general resemblance to Álvarez de Pineda's sketch map of the village of Francisco de Garay. This printed map shows the Gulf in a way quite similar to the Turin map that is said to be the work of Juan Vespucci. But none of the topography gives

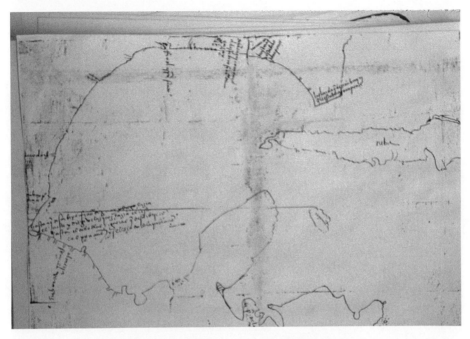

Plate 3.3. Alonso Álvarez de Pineda mapped the gulf coast in 1519. (Mapas y planos, Mexico 5.) Courtesy of the Ministerio de Educación y Cultura, Archivo General de Indias, Seville.

evidence of entradas other than those of Juan Ponce de León and Alonso Álvarez de Pineda.[22]

Several Spanish adventurers moved quickly to fill the gaps in American east coast geography. Pedro de Quejó sailed to the coast north of the earlier Spanish discoveries in the summer of 1521 on a slaving trip for Lucas Vázquez de Ayllón. In the next few years both men made trips to the mainland, to a province called Chicora.[23] This province was shown, with or without the name, in a number of maps drawn by official cartographers in Seville.

One of the earliest of these is the Castiglioni map, drawn in 1525 by Diego Ribero, one of the great cartographers in the Casa de Contratación.[24] The Castiglioni map is the first to show the 1525 journey of Esteban Gómez to the North American coast, well above the province visited by Quejó and Vázquez de Ayllón. This map is

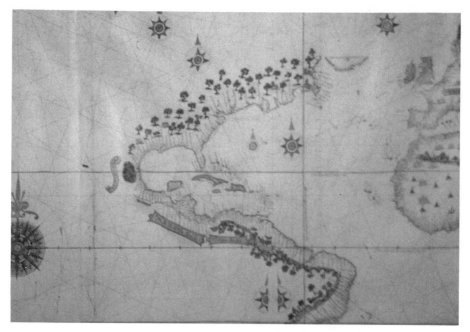

Plate 3.4. The "Salviati Map" of about 1525 is often attributed to Nuño García de Toreno. Photo courtesy of the Biblioteca Medicea Laurenziana, Florence.

now in the Archivio Marchesi Castiglioni in Mantua, said to have been a gift from Charles V to Count Baldassare Castiglioni, papal ambassador to the imperial court.[25]

A second map copied from the padrón real has been attributed by some to Nuño García de Toreno (ca. 1525). Now housed in the Biblioteca Medicea-Laurenziana at Florence, this map also shows the land explored by Gómez and Vázquez de Ayllón (plate 3.4). It is called the Salviati Planisphere because it was given by Charles V to Cardinal Ciovanni Salviati, when he came to Spain as apostolic nuncio in 1526.[26]

Several other world maps, certainly or very likely the work of Diego Ribero, still exist, and each of these shows the advance of Spanish exploration on the North American continent. Two of these maps are in the Thuringische Landesbibliothek at Weimar, the former Archducal Library.[27] Another Ribero world map, more famous than

Plate 3.5. Detail from the 1529 world map of Diego Ribero, perhaps the most beautiful of the Spanish maps of the sixteenth century. Borgiano 3. Photo courtesy of the Biblioteca Vaticana, Rome.

these and no doubt the most beautiful cartographic work produced in the Casa de Contratación, is in the Vatican Library (Borgiano 3) (plate 3.5).[28]

A map published in an anonymous work of 1534 is clearly based on the padrón real of Nuño García de Toreno (plate 3.6).[29] The book itself is variously attributed to Peter Martyr, who wrote much of the original text, or to Giovanni Ramusio, who helped arrange it for publication.[30] Unfortunately, there is little detail, and the map does not tell us much beyond the fact that the name Florida was applied to land above the peninsula as well as to the peninsula itself.

Even so, it does depict the state of the padrón real at the time of the first major entrada to the northern gulf coast. Organized in Spain by Pánfilo de Narváez, the fleet of five ships left Spain in June 1527 and landed on the gulf coast of Florida in April 1528. Perhaps the crowning blow in an astonishing series of near-disasters was the

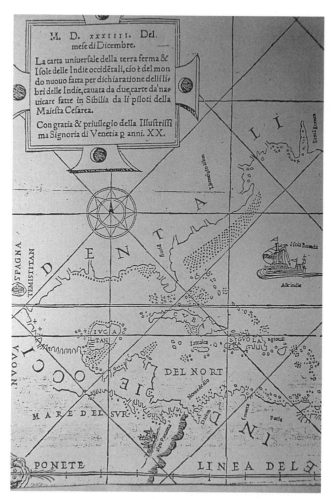

Plate 3.6. Detail of a map of America and the Atlantic Ocean printed in 1534, drawn from the work of Nuño García de Toreno. Courtesy of the John Carter Brown Library, Brown University, Providence, Rhode Island.

failure of the navigator, Diego Miruelo,[31] to land the force on the proper side of the bay, which nonetheless was named for him.[32]

Reduced to half its original size, the force of soldiers and colonists trudged through the woods and swamps until they reached the coast again at a large bay. Here the desperate men managed to turn their clothing and weapons into materials for construction of bargelike vessels, which they sailed and rowed westward along the coast past the mouth of the Mississippi. Early in November a single boatload of survivors was cast ashore on a Texas island. Enslaved for a time by Indians, the numbers of survivors dwindled until 1536, when four men, including Alvar Núñez Cabeza de Vaca, arrived at Culiacán on the west coast of New Spain, having marched clear across the plains of Texas and Mexico to reach a Spanish settlement.[33]

The map of Sebastian Cabot, printed at Nuremburg in 1544,[34] shows the Narváez landing place, the Baya de Miruelo, located just west of the point where the Florida peninsula joins the mainland and well north of the bay marked for Juan Ponce de León (plate 3.7).[35] The notation on the map says this is the "Bay of Miruelo, where Pánfilo de Narváez disembarked" (b. de miruelo aqui disen-barco panfilo de narnaez [sic]). A similar notation appears on two other maps thought to have been based on the copy of the padrón real prepared by Alonso de Chávez in 1536.[36] Whether the bay was the actual landing place is unclear, but it is almost certainly the place where Miruelo thought the expedition had landed, and it was certainly the location he gave to Fernández de Oviedo and to the pilots and cosmographers in the Casa de Contratación.[37]

It is possible to date the manuscript source of the Cabot map with some precision. The Cabot map does not contain any of the new information from the expedition of Hernando de Soto, from the voyages of Hernando de Alarcón and Francisco de Bolaños, or from the map of Domingo del Castillo. It does, however, have locations from the voyage of Francisco de Ulloa. For these reasons the date of the Cabot source map should be no earlier than 1540 and no later than early 1541. It would be logical to suppose that the source map was ready before Cabot signed the contract with his printers in March 1541.[38]

The astonishing trek of Cabeza de Vaca across the continent and his reasoned call for conversion of the Indians by preaching to them about the God of kindness and love, plus his veiled references to rich kingdoms yet unseen, rekindled Spanish interest in the northern territories. Cabeza de Vaca hoped to return to the country he had traversed, but before he could get back to Spain, Soto managed to

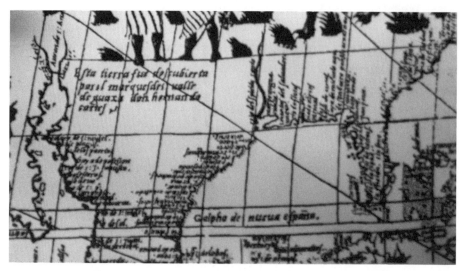

Plate 3.7. Sebastian Cabot's world map, printed in Nuremberg in 1544, shows the landing place of the Narváez expedition, the Baya de Miruelo. (Res.Ge.AA.582.) Courtesy of the Bibliothèque Nationale, Paris.

secure royal approval for his own colonization scheme.[39] Soto was to settle in a location of his choice in the vast country lying between northern New Spain and the Chicora region explored by Lucas Vázquez de Ayllón. All of this country was renamed Florida.[40]

Landing perhaps on Tampa Bay, Soto took his party through the northern part of the peninsula, then west along the coast. Turning inland, they marched into the Carolina region, then west across the Appalachian mountains. Crossing the Mississippi River, they trudged through Arkansas before returning to the river where the commander died. Repeating the experience of Narváez, the survivors constructed boats and made their way across the gulf to New Spain, where they arrived in September 1543.[41]

If the expedition was a failure in most ways, it resulted in major cartographic advances. The *cosmógrafo mayor* (royal cosmographer) Alonso de Santa Cruz drew a map of the region, showing most of the main Indian towns visited and the rivers traversed by the explorers (plate 3.8). Dated about 1544, the Santa Cruz map is generally con-

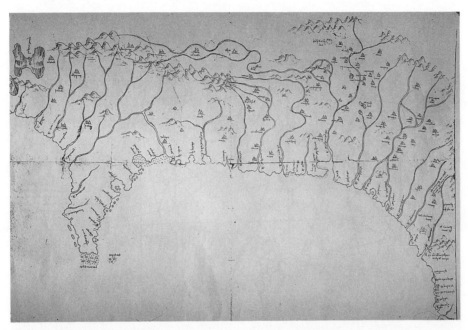

Plate 3.8. The earliest map to show the places visited by Hernando de Soto is the one drawn about 1544 by Alonso de Santa Cruz. (Mapas y planos, Mexico 1.) Courtesy of the Ministerio de Educación y Cultura, Archivo General de Indias, Seville.

sidered to be the first attempt to depict the interior of the present United States, using information from firsthand reports.[42]

The maps of Alonso de Santa Cruz and Sebastian Cabot have remarkably similar coastlines for Florida and the gulf coast, and most of the names of the rivers and bays are the same. Retaining the coastal features from the earlier padrón, Santa Cruz simply added interior details from Soto's expedition.[43] He retained the *b. de miruelo*, as did the later Spanish cosmographers, an indication of the confidence they had in the information given them by the pilot Diego Miruelo. This is in sharp contrast to the opinion of Cabeza de Vaca that "Miruelo did not know how to guide them to the port that the armada was hunting for, nor could he say where he left them nor where they were."[44]

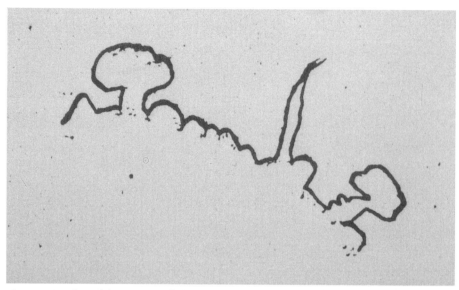

Plate 3.9. The oldest map of the west coast is this sketch of the shoreline in the bay at Santiago, Mexico, drawn by Alvaro de Saavedra Cerón in his report of 1527. (Patronato 43, no. 2, ramo. 4.) Courtesy of the Ministerio de Educación y Cultura, Archivo General de Indias, Seville.

Spanish exploration of the western part of North America came about largely as an outgrowth of the drive to find a sea route to the Spice Islands. When the survivors of the expeditions of Ferdinand Magellan, García Jofre de Loaysa, and Sebastian Cabot failed to return home, the Spanish king wrote to Hernán Cortés on June 20, 1527, and told him to send an expedition from the west coast of Mexico to find the lost Spaniards.[45]

Eager to trade with Asia, Cortés first sent out Alvaro de Saavedra Cerón to look for a better port for docking his fleet. This resulted in the discovery of the port of Santiago, which for several years served as a major port on the coast of Colima. The map that accompanied his report is also the oldest surviving map of any portion of the west coast of North America (plate 3.9).[46] Unfortunately, when Saavedra set out on his major voyage across the Pacific, his ships also joined the ranks of those lost in the islands of the Pacific. However, other ships did find land much closer to home. The place, at first thought to be an island, quickly came to be called California.[47]

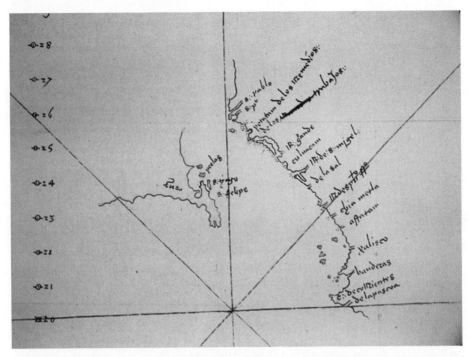

Plate 3.10. The first map to show settlements in California is this one of about 1539 filed with a legal case initiated by Hernán Cortés. (Mapas y planos, Mexico 6.) Courtesy of the Ministerio de Educación y Cultura, Archivo General de Indias, Seville.

The earliest map of this new land is a manuscript in the Archivo de Indias, drawn to accompany legal papers filed by the attorneys for Hernán Cortés in about 1539 (plate 3.10). This map is the first to show a European settlement on the peninsula, the town of Santa Cruz (now La Paz), founded by Cortés in 1535[48] but abandoned shortly thereafter.

A Spanish atlas finished by Bartolomé Olives in 1562 contains a map of North America that shows the peninsula settlement and other results of the early Ulloa voyages (plate 3.11). The information in the map is probably not later than 1540. All of the area north of New Spain is called Terra Florida, no doubt reflecting the expansion of Florida in the royal contract with Hernando de Soto.[49]

In 1541 Domingo del Castillo mapped both coasts of the peninsula and the west coast of New Spain, combining information from

Plate 3.11. Bartolomé Olives drew this map showing the Spanish view of North America in 1540. (Ms.Urb.Lat.283.) Photo courtesy of the Biblioteca Vaticana, Rome.

the 1539 expedition of Francisco de Ulloa and the 1541 expeditions of Hernando de Alarcón and Francisco de Bolaños. The Castillo map is now known only through an eighteenth-century copy, but there is some reason to think the copy was done with care and precision (plate 3.12).[50] As was the case with Florida, the name California was first applied to an island, but within a year or two was given to the tip of the peninsula, which is where it appears on this map. The name was applied much later to the entire peninsula and the country northward as well.[51]

The maps of Alonso de Santa Cruz and Sebastian Cabot also reflect the uncertainty in the Casa de Contratación about new information arriving from the west coast of New Spain. The map printed for Cabot in 1544 is important because it reflects the state of knowledge about the peninsula after Ulloa completed his expedition but before 1541, when the Castillo map was made. The Santa Cruz maps of 1542 give a totally different view of the peninsula, bisected

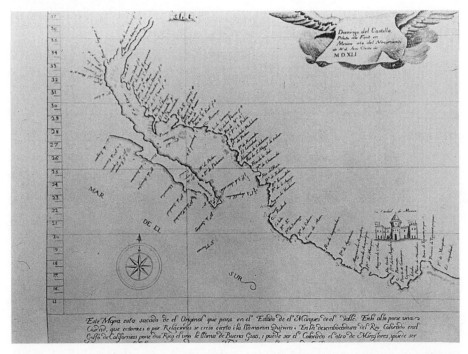

Plate 3.12. Domingo del Castillo drew a map of the west coast in 1541; the only surviving copy appears to be this one made in the eighteenth century. In *Historia de Neuva España, escrita por su esclarecida conquistador Hernán Cortés*, by Francisco Antonio Lorenzana (Mexico City: Imprenta del Supremo Gobierno, 1770). Courtesy of the DeGolyer Library, Southern Methodist University, Dallas.

to create an island at the southern tip, perhaps a misunderstanding of some of the geography reported by Ulloa.[52] His men had noted the deep bays on both sides of the peninsula and wondered whether they might really be straits.[53]

Several small fleets sailed up the gulf in 1540 and 1541. One of the most important was that of Alarcón, who was supposed to establish contact with the overland expedition of Francisco Vázquez de Coronado. Alarcón ascended a river that he named Río de Buena Guía (Colorado River). He claimed to have gone four degrees farther than Ulloa and to have been eighty-five leagues up the river, but this seems like an exaggeration. In any case, he did not meet the overland party and did little else except confirm the geography described by Ulloa and his lieutenant, Francisco Preciado.[54]

The exact route taken by Vázquez de Coronado's expedition has been a matter of dispute for years,[55] with resolution still so far away that historians have begun to wonder instead whether he should have gone at all.[56] Perhaps moved by Cabeza de Vaca's plea for a peaceful entrada, Viceroy Antonio de Mendoza named Fray Marcos de Niza to scout the route in 1539, guided by Estevánico, a dark-skinned Moor who had been with Cabeza de Vaca.[57] Catching a distant view of the Zuñi pueblos, Fray Marcos decided he had seen the Seven Cities of myth, somehow transferred from their location in the Atlantic Ocean, and hurried home to report his find.[58]

Encouraged by the reports, Vázquez de Coronado hastened out in 1540 to the interior of North America. The Cíbola he found was not very grand, but he brought back information about the Indian towns at Zuñi, the Hopi towns, and the pueblos along the Rio Grande. Picking up Indian guides from Pecos, he marched eastward to the Great Plains called Quivira, where Indians followed the buffalo herds. Scouting parties from his expedition reached the Grand Canyon and the delta of the Colorado River, while one friar and two Indian lay brothers made a long, lonely trek overland through Texas and back to the Gulf of Mexico. All this information was added to the newest Spanish maps, though the exact locations of some of the places varied from map to map.[59]

The 1542 "Stockholm map" by Alonso de Santa Cruz alludes to the expedition with a note that the land was under exploration by order of Antonio de Mendoza.[60] A legend on the North America map in the Santa Cruz *Islario general* locates the Seven Cities (*las siete ciudades*) but does not mention Quivira or depict the buffalo. This indicates that when he drew these maps Santa Cruz knew about Niza's travels but perhaps did not know the results of the Vázquez de Coronado expedition. So the information on the North America maps by Santa Cruz can be dated about 1539 or 1540.[61] The "De Soto map" by Santa Cruz does make a reference to discoveries of the Vázquez de Coronado expedition. A notation along the western edge gives a brief mention of Quivira and the buffalo herds: "desde quevira hasta aqui ay grandisimas manadas de vacas" (From Quivira to here there are huge herds of cattle), thus confirming the date of this map at about 1544.

The most colorful Spanish map of this period is the one by Sancho Gutiérrez, dated 1551. Now in the Österreichische National-bibliothek in Vienna,[62] this map is one of the earliest to depict the North American bison. The Gutiérrez map is based on the same copy of the padrón real as that of Olives, but the Gutiérrez map shows later information as well as a note that "Cabeza de Vaca went this way."[63] Unfortunately, this portion of the Gutiérrez map is badly waterstained, and it is no longer possible to discern other information about the Vázquez de Coronado and Soto expeditions.[64]

Quite possibly there was no more information. Certainly the map has nothing about the 1542 expedition of Juan Rodríguez Cabrillo to the coast of Upper California and the northwest. The earliest map to show this information is a copy of the padrón real made in 1559 by Andrés Homem (plate 3.13).[65] Using supplemental information and perhaps maps of the Cabrillo expedition supplied in the 1550s by Fray Andrés de Urdaneta,[66] Homem showed ports and bays named by Cabrillo but did not include Indian towns on the coast. The Homem copy of the padrón real shows several interior provinces visited by the expedition of Hernando de Soto. "Chicapro" is undoubtedly Chisca Provincia; "Cosapro" is Coça Provincia, lying to the south. "Terra Florida" covers all the country to the east; a mysterious "Svagra" lies to the west. This may be an abbreviation for Çivola Granada, the names applied by the Vázquez de Coronado expedition to the village of Hawikuh.[67] This place-name is in the same general location on the Homem map as the siete ciudades on the Santa Cruz map of North America in the *Islario general*.

Cabrillo explored the coast of present-day California, established a camp on Catalina Island, and wrote a description of the coast. His expedition, part of a two-pronged attempt to reach the Spice Islands and China, reflected a continuing belief that North America might possibly be joined to Asia. The plan was for the Cabrillo fleet to

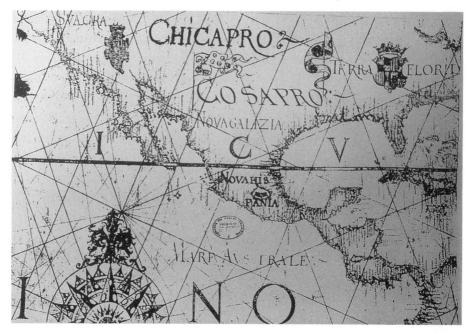

Plate 3.13. Andrés Homem made this copy of the official Spanish padrón in 1559, showing the coastal places visited by Cabrillo and the provinces of Chisca and Coça, among others visited by the Vásquez de Coronado expedition. (Res.Ge.CC.2719.) Courtesy of the Bibliothèque Nationale, Paris.

reach Asia by following the coast north and west. Another fleet commanded by Ruy López de Villalobos was to sail directly west.

The question of whether a strait existed was partly settled in 1561 when Giacomo Gastaldi misread the account of Marco Polo's journey. Thinking the Venetian traveler had already found such a strait, Gastaldi placed the Strait of Anian on his new printed map of the world.[68] For many years historians considered the 1562 North America map made by Diego Gutiérrez to be the earliest printed map bearing the name California. Actually, the first was this 1561 map by Gastaldi, though both of the maps were probably drawing information from the same copy of the padrón real.[69] The earliest manuscript map with the name California is probably the ca. 1540 map of North America in the 1562 Olives atlas (plate 3.14, page 103).[70]

North American place-names and locations are very nearly the same on both the Gastaldi and the Diego Gutiérrez maps, and both were based on a copy of the padrón real made before 1554, when Gutiérrez died. Because Gastaldi located Quivira on the Pacific Coast, it seems likely that this was the location of Quivira on the padrón real in the early 1550s. Thus the cosmographers of the Casa de Contratación, rather than Battista Agnese and Francisco López de Gómara, may have been responsible for transferring Quivira from Kansas to California.[71]

Spanish activities on the east coast were renewed in 1565 when Pedro Menéndez de Avilés led another expedition to explore, settle, and defend the provinces of Florida. Saint Augustine was founded in September 1565, and in the following year another settlement was established on present-day Parris Island. Called Santa Elena, this town was the key to later penetrations of the interior. In late 1566 Juan Pardo began a series of journeys into present South Carolina, Georgia, and Alabama, founding Spanish towns and forts at the Indian towns of Guatari and Joada. Other forts and settlements were established in the peninsula, including Tocobaga, formerly the Baya de Miruelo.[72]

A third North American map by Alonso de Santa Cruz dated about 1566 is perhaps the earliest to locate the river of San Agustino. It was no doubt drawn within a year or so of the time when Menéndez de Avilés established a fortified settlement there in 1565. There are two lakes in the interior, one of which bears the name *coniu[nctu]s lacus*. At the east side of this lake is the notation *nuevo mexico* and at the top a note that the latitude is about 54°.[73] Sometimes said to be a depiction of the Great Lakes, based on Indian accounts, it could just as logically be called a map of the Great Salt Lake, with a swampy Utah Lake to the south.

The renewed Spanish interest in La Florida can he seen in the ca. 1574 geographic study of the Indies by Juan López de Velasco, but his map of the region is not satisfactory (plate 3.15).[74] Another map that possibly dates from about 1595 shows more detail, but the authorship is uncertain.[75]

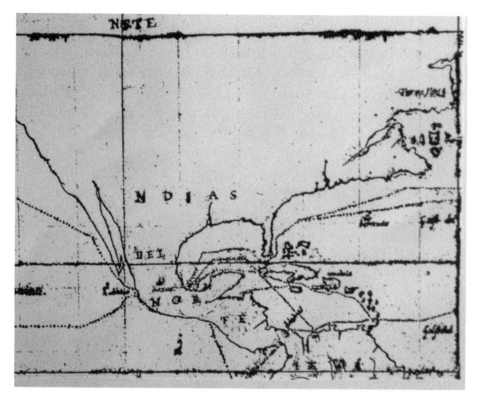

Plate 3.15. Juan López de Velasco sketched this rough drawing of North America about 1574. Courtesy of the John Carter Brown Library, Brown University, Providence, Rhode Island.

In New Spain settlement pushed rapidly northward, drawn by mineral discoveries in the central plateau region. By 1580 settlement had reached Santa Bárbara in Chihuahua. In 1581 a small group of Franciscans led by Fray Augustín Rodríguez determined to carry the gospel to new mission fields. Escorted by Captain Francisco Sánchez Chamuscado and a few soldiers, the party marched north to the Pueblo region of the Rio Grande Valley.

This initial group was followed in late 1582 by a relief party under Antonio de Espejo. Returning a year later, Espejo made a glowing report of all he had seen and done. As a result, the Spanish king issued a royal order to establish a permanent settlement in New

Mexico and bring the Indians under control of the Crown. There was much discussion in New Spain, but little action until 1598, when Juan de Oñate led his first group of settlers to the Rio Grande Valley.

One of the men who went with Oñate was an experienced mariner named Juan Rodríguez, who returned to Mexico in 1602. Rodríguez brought with him geographic information so detailed that a cosmographer was able to draw a map of the region. Now in the Archivo de Indias, this map by Enrico Martínez is the oldest surviving map to show the interior of Cíbola with any accuracy.[76]

By the end of the century the work of the great pilots and cosmographers in the Casa de Contratación seemed to have produced the desired result. From the first there had been disputes about the accuracy of one or another of the successive versions of the padrón real. Yet the work continued, drawing on the experience of practical navigators, who kept their own charts up to date, even when their results were not accepted in the padrón real. And though their main interest was not the interior of the country, these navigators and mapmakers managed to inform their countrymen and the rest of the world about the astonishing things that existed in this strange New World.

NOTES

Research for this paper was made possible by grants from the American Philosophical Society, the Giles W. and Elise G. Mead Foundation, the Huntington Library, and the Newberry Library

1. Harry Kelsey, "The Planispheres of Sebastian Cabot and Sancho Gutiérrez," *Terrae Incognitae* 19 (1987):48–51.

2. Ernesto Schäfer, *El Consejo Real y Supremo de las Indias: Su historia, organización y labor administrativa hasta la terminación de la Casa de Austria*, 2 vols. (Seville: Universidad de Sevilla and Escuela de Estudios Hispano-Americanos, 1935–47), 1:10.

3. Peter Martyr, *De orbe novo Petri Martyris ab Angleria* (Alcala: Michael de Eguia, 1530), decada 2, libro 10, December 1514, fols. 35–36.

Manuel de la Puente y Olea, *Los trabajos geográficos de la Casa de Contratación* (Seville: Escuela Tipográfica y Librería Salesianas, 1900), 254, 274.

4. Vespucci was named to the post on March 22, 1508. See Ernesto Schäfer, *Consejo Real*, 1:21. The first page of the *cédula* (decree) appointing him piloto mayor (Archivo General de Indias, Indiferente General 1961) is reproduced by Alberto Giraldi in his *Raccolta di carte e documenti esposti alla mostra tenuta in Palazzo Vechio a Firenze nel V Centenial della nascita del Amerigo Vespucci* (Milan: Amilcari Pizzi, 1955), pl. 5. The text was transcribed and printed by Martín Fernández de Navarrete in his *Colección de los viajes y descubrimientos que hicieron por mar los Españoles desde fines del siglo XV* (Madrid: Imprenta y Librería de Moya y Plaza, 1880), 301–5.

5. [Martin Waldseemüller], *Cosmographiae introductio cum quibusdam geometriae ac astronomicae principiis ad eam rem necessariis insuper quatuor Americi Vespucii navigationes* (St. Dié: Gymnasium Vosagense, 1507), caput 9. The bibliographic questions on this work are explained by José Alberto Aboal Amaro, *Amerigho Vespucci: Ensayo de bibliografía crítica* (Madrid: Librería para Bibliófilos, 1962), 40–41.

6. Gonzalo Fernández de Oviedo, *Libro .XX. De la segunda parte de la general historia de las Indias* (Valladolid: Francisco Fernández de Cordova, 1557), fol. v, verso: "fue grande ombre de la mar y sabio cosmographo." This material does not appear in his *Historia general y natural de las Indias* (Seville: Juan Cromberger, 1535), which has only 19 books, plus a "libro último" on a different subject. George Rithaymer used almost the same words in *De orbis terrarum situ compendium* (Nuremberg: Joannis Petreius, 1538), 111: "Americus Vesputius vir rerum maritimarum & astronicarum insigniter peritus." Fernández de Oviedo wrote this part of his work about 1539, so it is possible that he borrowed his wording from Rithaymer, since he may not have known Vespucci personally. Dating of the manuscript and printed versions is explained by Daymond Turner in "The Aborted First Printing of the Second Part of Oviedo's *General and Natural History of the Indies,*" *Huntington Library Quarterly* 46 (Spring 1983): 118–19, 125. The best modern edition of Oviedo's *Historia general* is the edition of the Biblioteca de Autores Españoles (Madrid: Ediciones Atlas, 1959), in which this appears as libro XX, capitulo I, 2:218; cited hereafter as BAE 2:218.

SPANISH ENTRADA CARTOGRAPHY

7. The King-Hamy portulano (HM 45) at the Huntington Library has been attributed to Amerigo Vespucci; see Giraldi, *Amerigo Vespucci*, pl. 10. The "Pesaro Map" of ca. 1505–08 at the Biblioteca e Musei Oliverani, Pesaro, Italy, has been cited as "a fairly good copy of Vespucci's 1508 *padrón*." See Edward L. Stevenson, "The Geographical Activities of the Casa de Contratación," *Annals of the Association of American Geographers* 17 (1927):43–51, quoted in Frederick J. Pohl, "The Pesaro Map, 1505," *Imago Mundi* 7 (1951):82–83. Puente y Olea, *Trabajos geográficos*, 276, 302–3, says the map is the work of Nuño García de Toreno. Margaret S. Dilke and A. Brancati show that recent research makes it difficult to accept any definite conclusion about the map; see their article, "The New World in the Pesaro Map," *Imago Mundi* 40 (1988):78–83.

8. The *real cédula* (royal decree) of July 24, 1512, is published in José Toribio Medina, *Juan Díaz de Solís: Estudio historico*, vol. 2, *Documentos* (Santiago de Chile: Impresso en Casa del Autor, 1897), 81–85.

9. For claims that the Cantino and Waldseemüller maps show early discoveries of Florida, see Jerald T. Milanich and Susan Milbrath, "Another World," in *First Encounters: Spanish Explorations in the Caribbean and the United States, 1492–1570*, edited by Jerald T. Milanich and Susan Milbrath (Gainesville: University of Florida Press and Florida Museum of Natural History, 1989), 11–12. An earlier expression of this opinion is found in William P. Cumming, *The Southeast in Early Maps* (Princeton: Princeton University Press, 1958), 6, 64–65. Most scholars do not accept this view. See, for example, Miguel León-Portilla, *Cartografía y crónicas de la Antigua California* (Mexico City: Universidad Nacional Autónoma de México, 1989), 23–30. See also Robert H. Fuson, "The John Cabot Mystique," in *Essays on the History of North American Discovery and Exploration*, edited by Stanley H. Palmer and Dennis Reinhartz (College Station: Texas A&M University Press, 1988), 51.

10. Antonio de Herrera, *Historia general de los hechos de los Castellanos en las islas y Tierra Firme del mar océano* (Madrid: Juan de la Cuesta, 1615), decada 2, libro 1, capitulo 12. Manuel de la Puente y Olea, *Trabajos geográficos de la Casa de Contratación* (Seville: Tipografica y Librería Salesianas, 1900), 281–82. Medina, *Juan Díaz de Solís*, 1:ccvii.

11. Arthur Davies, "The Egerton MS. 2803 Map and the Padrón Real of Spain in 1510," *Imago Mundi* 11 (1954):46–52.

12. Peter Martyr, *Opera. Legatio babilonica. Occeanea decas. Poemata* (Hispali: Jacobum Corumberger Aleman, 1511), leaf f.ix, Newberry Library. The map does not appear in every copy of the book, allegedly because the king ordered it to be withdrawn. See Diego Luís Molinari, *El nacimiento del Nuevo Mundo, 1492–1543* (Buenos Aires: Editorial Kapelusz, 1941), 64. Henry Wagner thought Molinari lacked firsthand proof for this statement. See his article, "Peter Martyr and His Work," American Antiquarian Society *Proceedings* 56 (October 1946):263, 265. The map is found in the Newberry Library copy but not in the copy at the Huntington Library. A copy of the book at the Biblioteca Columbina in Seville has an altogether different map pasted in the back, to judge from the very obscure photocopy deposited at the Huntington Library (R 126719).

13. Fernández de Oviedo, *Historia general*, primera parte, libro 16, capitulo 11, fol. cxxv; BAE 2:102.

14. Peter Martyr, *De orbe novo decadas* (Alcala: Antonius Nebrissensis, 1516), "crediti continenti," liber 10, sheet f. ii. Also in the later editions, *De orbe novo*, decada 2, libro 10, fol. 36.

15. Fernández de Oviedo's brief account of the journey is apparently from Juan Ponce de León himself, about whom Fernández de Oviedo said, "I knew him very well." In another reference to Ponce de León, Narváez, Garay, Vázquez de Ayllón, and Hernando de Soto, Oviedo said, "I knew them well and talked with them and corresponded with them." See the *Historia general*, primera parte, libro 16, capitulas 2, 4, and 9; libro 17, capitulo 25; BAE 2:89, 94, 102, 165. The main documents are cited and quoted briefly by Manuel Ballesteros Gaibrois, *La idea colonial de Ponce de León: Un ensayo de interpretación* (San Juan de Puerto Rico: Instituto de Cultura Puertorriqueña, 1960), esp. pp. 65–75, 116, 279, 290. The Ponce de León view of Florida as an island is seen in the "Wolfenbüttel Map" (ca. 1523–25), Aug. fol. 103, Herzog August Bibliothek, Wolfenbüttel; it has been attributed to Girolamo Verrazzano and Diego Ribero among others. For a reproduction, see *Alte Karten und Globen in der Herzog August Bibliothek, Wolfenbüttel* (Wolfenbüttel: Yorck Alexander Haase, 1972), 26–27.

16. If Álvarez de Pineda wrote a report, it is not known now, but his sketch map still exists in the Archivo de Indias, Mapas y Planos, Mexico 5, where there is also a real cédula, summarizing the report submitted by Francisco de Garay. A copy of the real cédula of 1521 and a good reprint of the map of ca. 1520 may be found in the work by Fernández de Navarrete, *Colección de los viajes*, 3:148–55; map opp. p. 148. Henry Harrisse explained the linkage between the map and the cédula in *Discovery of North America* (London, 1892; reprint Amsterdam: Nico Israel, 1969), 151–53.

17. Herrera, who may have had access to information not now available, describes the wound in his *Historia general*, decada 3, libro 1, capitulo 14.

18. The first inscription says, "La Florida q decian Bimini q descubrio Juan Ponce." The second says, "Hasta aq descubrio Juan Ponce."

19. "Y esto yo lo he visto (sin la fuente) no en el subjeto e mejoramiento delas fuerças, pero en el enflaquecimiento del seso, e tornar se en sus hechos mozos y de poco entender: y déstos fué uno el mismo joan ponce en tanto que le turo aquella vanidad de dar crédito a los indios en tal disparate." Oviedo, *Historia general*, primera parte, libro 16, capitulo 13, fol. cxxvi verso; BAE 2:105. For a more sympathetic view, see Ballesteros, *La idea colonial de Ponce de León*, 65–69, 103–6.

20. Alberto Magnaghi, *Il Planisfero del 1523 della Biblioteca del Re in Torino. La prima carta del mondo costruita dopo il viaggio di Magellano. Unica copia conosciuta di carta generale ad uso dei piloti dell'epoca delle grandi scoperte* (Florence: Lange, 1929), cited by Roberto Almagià, in his "Planisfero di Diego Ribero: Siviglia, 1929," *Planisferi, Carte Nautiche, e Affini dal secolo XIV al XVII esistenti nella Biblioteca Apostolica Vaticana* (Vatican City: Biblioteca Apostolica Vaticana, 1944), 51. There is a good color reproduction in Giraldi, *Amerigo Vespucci*, pl. 24.

21. Hernán Cortés, *Praeclara Fernandi Cortesii de Nova Maris Oceani Hyspania narratio* (Nuremberg: Conventum Imperialum, 1524), foldout map opp. fol. 1.

22. Paul E. Hoffman describes the ca. 1514–17 voyage of Pedro de Salazar to the Island of Giants as a nearly unrecorded and certainly unmapped early visit to the South Carolina coast. See his study, "A New

Voyage of North American Discovery: Pedro de Salazar's Visit to the 'Island of Giants,'" *Florida Historical Quarterly* 58 (April 1980): 415–26.

23. The real cédula of Vázquez de Ayllón, June 12, 1523, is reprinted by Navarrete in *Collección de viajes*, 3:155–64. Paul Hoffman has a detailed account of the Quejó-Vázquez de Ayllón matter in his book, *A New Andalucia and a Way to the Orient: The American Southeast during the Sixteenth Century* (Baton Rouge: Louisiana State University Press, 1990), 3–83.

24. The basic biographical information about Ribero is in a series of articles and documents written and assembled by German Latorre, "Diego Ribero: Cosmógrafo y cartógrafo de la Casa de Contratación de Sevilla," *Boletín del Centro de Estudios Americanistas* 5 (November 1918): 27–31; 5 (December 1918):18–35.

25. Armando Cortesão, "Note on the Castiglione Planisphere," *Imago Mundi* 11 (1954):53–56, including a foldout reproduction of the map. Cortesão is less certain about the authorship of the map than Luís A. Vigneras; see Vigneras, "The Cartographer Diogo Ribeiro," *Imago Mundi* 16 (1962): 78.

26. Puente y Olea, *Trabajos geográficos*, 303–5. The map is dated no later than 1526, the year Nuño García de Toreno died (ibid., 297). The Biblioteca Medicea Laurenziana dates the map (Med. Palat. 249) at "about 1525." See *Monumenta di Cartografia a Firenze (Secc. X–XVII)*, IX Conferenza Internazzionale di Storia della Cartografia (Florence: Biblioteca Medicea Laurenziana, 1981), 43.

27. Johann G. Kohl, *Die Beiden Ältesten General-Karten von Amerika ausgeführt in den jahren 1527 und 1529 auf BJefehl Kaiser Karl's V. im Besitz der Grossherzoglichen Bibliothek zu Weimar* (Weimar: Geographisches Institut, 1860).

28. Once part of the permanent display in the Vatican Museum, the map is now faded and does not reproduce well. A readable contemporary copy can be seen in Roberto Almagiá, *Planisferi, carte nautiche e affini dal secolo XIV al XVII esistenti nella Biblioteca Apostolica Vaticana* (Vatican City: Bibliteca Apostolica Vaticana, 1944), pls. 21–23. There is a fine reproduction of the original state of this map in the copy published by W. Griggs at London in ca. 1886. See Rodney W. Shirley,

The Mapping of the World: Early Printed World Maps, 1472–1700 (London: Holland Press, 1983), xxiv–xxv. This and other Ribero maps are reproduced in large format by Armando Cortesão and Avelino Teixeira Da Mota in *Portugaliae Monumenta Cartographica*, 5 vols. (Lisbon: n.p., 1960), 1:pls. 37–41. A recent reproduction of the Wolfenbüttel map can be seen in *Alte Karten und Globen in der Herzog August Bibliothek, Wolfenbüttel*, 26–27.

29. *Libro primo de la historia de l'Indie Occidentali* (Venice: n.p., 1534). There is an original copy of the map at the John Carter Brown Library (Cabinet B 534 1), and though it is not inserted in the book, the text of libro 2, fol. 64, clearly refers to this map.

30. Lawrence Wroth, *Report to the Corporation of Brown University, July 1, 1929* (Providence: John Carter Brown Library, 1929), 25–28. George B. Parks, "Columbus and Balboa in the Italian Revision of Peter Martyr," *Huntington Library Quarterly* 18 (June 1955): 209–12.

31. Diego Miruelo is a shadowy figure. The available biographical information is summarized by Robert S. Weddle, *Spanish Sea: The Gulf of Mexico in North American Discovery, 1500–1685* (College Station: Texas A&M University Press, 1985), 204–5.

32. Fernández de Oviedo, *Historia general*, primera parte, libro 16, capitulos 1, 8; segunda parte, libro 21, capitulo 8; BAE 2:332, 4:288–315. Presumably he returned to Mexico with the fleet and later provided Fernández de Oviedo and others with information about the bays along the coast, as pilots were required to do.

33. "Relacion de cabeza de vaca thesorero q fue en la conquista," AGI, Patronato 20, no. 5, ramo 3. Translated by Frederick W. Hodge as "The Narrative of Alvar Nuñez Cabeça de Vaca," *Spanish Explorers in the Southern United States, 1528–1543* (New York: Charles Scribner's Sons, 1907), 12–126.

34. Res. Ge. AA. 582, Départment des Cartes et Plans, Bibliothèque Nationale, Paris. The map has been reproduced many times, but detail is often obscured. A recent color reproduction was issued by Roger Hervè, André Rossel, and Jeanne Sorozabal Kirschen under the title *Mappemonde de Sébastien Cabot, piloto major de Charles-Quint—Governeur de la Compagnie des Adventuriers-marchands, 1544* (Paris: Editions les Yeux

Ouverts, Livre Club Diderot, 1968). There are also large photostatic copies in many American research libraries.

35. Spanish cosmographers continued to distinguish between the Baya de Miruelo and the Baya de Juan Ponce, both on maps and in their geographic commentaries. See the comments of the sixteenth-century cosmógrafo mayor Alonso de Chávez, written before 1538, *Quatri partitu en cosmografía practica, y por otro nombre espejo de navegantes* (Madrid: Instituto de Historia y Cultura Naval, 1983), 364–66; and the similar study completed by Juan López de Velasco in 1574, *Geografía y descripción universal de las Indias*, vol. 248 of Bibliteca de Autores Españoles (Madrid: Ediciones Atlas, 1971), 85. Considering their work and the plain testimony of the maps it is difficult to see how Woodbury Lowery arrived at his decision that the Bay of Miruelo was Tampa Bay. Lowery, *Spanish Settlements within the Present Limits of the United States: Florida, 1562–1574* (New York: G. P. Putnam's Sons, 1905), 448–50. Following Lowery, John R. Swanton decided that the Baya de Miruelo and the Baya de Juan Ponce were both Tampa Bay. See his *Final Report of the United States De Soto Expedition Commission* (Washington, D.C., Smithsonian Institution, 1985 reprint), 109–38.

36. These are the North America maps in the anonymous world atlas, MS. 129.A.24, fols. 23v–24, Koninklijke Bibliotheek, The Hague; and the "Harleian Map," Add. MS. 5413, British Library, London. In both maps, however, the delineation of the Florida coast varies somewhat from that shown in the Cabot map.

37. One possible reason historians ignore the Baya de Miruelo is that is has been difficult to find a readable copy of the Cabot map. See, for example, Buckingham Smith, who saw the Jomard reproduction of the map with its erroneous reading of the place-name and thought it too ridiculous to take seriously: *Relation of Alvar Nuñez Cabeça de Vaca, Translated from the Spanish* (New York: Estate of Buckingham Smith, 1871), 56.

38. Henry Wagner thought the Sebastian Cabot map reflected the state of the padrón real in 1541–42: *Cartography of the Northwest Coast of America to the Year 1800*, 2 vols. (Amsterdam: N. Israel, 1968; reprint of the 1937 edition), 1:24. The Cabot contract is in Seville, Archivo de Protocolos, oficio 1, año 1541, libro 1, fol. 575; reprinted in José Toribio

Medina, *El Veneciano, Sebastián Caboto al servicio de España y especialmente de su proyectado viaje á las Molucas por el Estrecho de Magallanes y al reconocimiento de la costa del continente hasta la gobernación de Pedrarías Dávila*, 2 vols. (Santiago de Chile: Imprenta y Encuadernación Universitaria, 1903), 1:555–57.

39. Cyclone Covey, trans. and ed., *Cabeza de Vaca's Adventures in the Unknown Interior of America* (Albuquerque: University of New Mexico Press, 1961), 12–14.

40. Hoffman, *New Andalucia*, 58, 87–88.

41. Ibid., 90–96. Luís Fernández de Viedma, Relación de la ysla de la florida, AGI, Patronato 19, ramo 3.

42. The map is in AGI, Mapas y Planos, Mexico No. 1. Described in Cumming, *The Southeast in Early Maps*, 94. A more complete analysis can be found in David Buisseret's article, "Spanish and French Mapping of the Gulf of Mexico in the Sixteenth and Seventeenth Centuries," in *The Mapping of the American Southwest*, edited by Dennis Reinhartz and Charles Colley (College Station: Texas A&M University Press, 1987).

43. Jeffrey P. Bain called attention to the coastline delineation in his "Introduction: Update of De Soto Studies since the United States De Soto Expedition Commission Report," in the reprint of John P. Swanton's *Final Report of the United States De Soto Expedition Commission*, xi–lvi, esp. fn. 6, p. 1.

44. Fernández de Oviedo had his information from Cabeza de Vaca and his companions through copies of the official reports he received in 1539, supplemented by personal interviews to 1547; *Historia general*, segunda parte, libro 35, capitulos 6, 7; BAE, 4:314–15.

45. The document is printed in the documentary collections of Arturo Basílio de Sá, ed., *Documentação para a história das missões do padroado Português do Oriente*, vol. 1, *Insulindia 1506–1549* (Lisbon: Agência Geral do Ultramar, Divisão de Publicaçoes e Biblioteca, 1954), 212–17.

46. *Relacion del viage q. hizo un bergantin en lo de la mar del sur antes que enbieron los navios*, AGI, Patronato 43, no. 2, ramo 4.

47. Harry E. Kelsey, "Mapping the California Coast: The Voyages of Discovery," *Arizona and the West* 26 (Winter 1984): 307–11.

48. AGI, Mapas y Planos, Mexico 6. The map is sometimes dated 1535 because of a notation on an insert sheet in AGI, Patronato 21, no. 2, ramo 4, fol. 10, which says that the map was transferred to another file but that it depicts the land discovered by Cortés on May 3, 1535. There is a fine-looking reproduction in León-Portilla, *Cartografía y crónicas de la Antigua California*, opp. p. 48. Unfortunately, this illustration appears to have been taken from the modern copy in the Museo Naval at Madrid, on which the name of the town has been transcribed as a nearly illegible "cruz."

49. Biblioteca Apostolica Vaticana, MS. Urb. Lat. 283. There is a microfilm copy of this and other Vatican Library materials in the Vatican Film Library, Saint Louis University. The atlas is described in Almagiá, *Planisferi carte nautiche e affini*, 72–75. Henry Wagner called this "the earliest known Spanish atlas to display the discoveries of Ulloa and Alarcón." See his *Cartography of the Northwest Coast*, 38. The Olives maps are very similar to the 1551 Sancho Gutiérrez world map in Vienna, which is very likely an older map redecorated in 1551.

50. The map is in Francisco Antonio Lorenzana, *Historia de Nueva España escrita por su esclarecida conquistador Hernán Cortés* (Mexico: Imprenta del Supremo Gobierno, 1770), 328. Ernest J. Burrus commented on the accuracy of the map in *Kino and the Cartography of Northwestern New Spain* (Tucson: Arizona Pioneers Historical Society, 1965), 30 n 3. As Burrus notes, Humboldt saw the original map in the Cortés family archives; he discussed both the original and the copy as though there were no appreciable difference. See his *Ensayo político sobre el reino de la Nueva España*, edición crítica por Vito Alessio Robles, 5 vols. (Mexico: D. F. Robredo, 1941), 1:162, 185. León-Portilla published a map drawn by the staff at the Museo Naval in the mistaken belief that it was "a later copy of the original" Castillo map. See his *Cartografía y crónicas de la Antigua California*, 43.

51. The name California was applied to an island in the bay at Santa Cruz in 1541, according to testimony by Fray Antonio de Meno. Mexico, Archivo General de la Nación, Hospital de Jesús, leg. 300, exp. 114, fol. 116. When Juan Rodríguez Cabrillo went there in 1542, he applied the name to a point at the southern end of the peninsula. Harry

Kelsey, *Juan Rodríguez Cabrillo* (San Marino, Calif.: Huntington Library, 1986), 123–28.

52. The map in question is entitled *Novus verior et integra totius orbis descriptio nunc primum in lucem edita per Alfonsum de Sancta Cruz Caesaris Charoli .V. archicosmographum .A.D.M.D.xlii*, world map on vellum, Kunglia Bibliotheket, Stockholm, Sweden. It was reproduced in portfolio by E. W. Dahlgren, *Map of the World by the Spanish Cosmographer, Alonzo de Santa Cruz, 1542* (Stockholm: Royal Printing Office, 1892). There is a similar map in the *Islario general de todas las islas del mundo*, also done by Santa Cruz, which exists in nearly identical manuscripts at the Biblioteca del Palacio Real in Madrid and the Österreichische Nationalbibliothek in Vienna. A third copy of the manuscript in the Bibliotheque de Besançon, France (Coll. Chiflet, MS. vol. 67), lacks the maps. The name of Santa Cruz was later obliterated from the title page of the Madrid copy, but the identity of the author was established by Antonio Blasquez, who published the manuscript and indifferent reproductions of the maps in *Islario general de todas las islas del mundo*, 2 vols. (Madrid: Imprenta del Patronato de Huérfanos de Intendencia de Intervención Militares, 1918). A fine color reproduction of the North American portion is found in León-Portilla, mislabeled as a copy of the Stockholm map. León-Portilla, *Cartografía y crónicas de la Antigua California*, lamina XII, opp. p. 52.

53. Ulloa's relación is found in AGI, Patronato 20, no. 5, ramo 11. There is a good translation by Irene A. Wright in Henry Wagner's *Spanish Voyages to the Northwest Coast of America in the Sixteenth Century* (San Francisco: California Historical Society, 1929), 15–50. The Preciado account, published by Giovanni Battista Ramusio in his *Terzo volume della navigatione et viaggi* (Venice: Stamperia di Giunti, 1565), fols. 341–43, has several references to the failure to see whether the bays might have been straits. The account by Alarcón is on fols. 363–70; there is a translation by George P. Hammond and Agapito Rey in *Narratives of the Coronado Expedition, 1540–42*, vol. 2 of *Coronado Cuarto Centennial Publications, 1540–1950* (Albuquerque: University of New Mexico Press, 1940), 124–55.

54. Ramusio, *Terzo volume della navigatione et viaggi*, fols. 341–43, 363–70. The Alarcón account is translated by George P. Hammond and

Agapito Rey in *Narratives of the Coronado Expedition, 1540–42,* 2:124–55.

55. John L. Kessell outlines the general problem in his foreword to the reprint edition of Herbert E. Bolton's *Coronado: Knight of Pueblos and Plains* (Albuquerque: University of New Mexico Press, 1990), xiii–xxiv.

56. David J. Weber is probably the most eloquent of this group. See his "Reflections on Coronado and the Myth of Quivira," in Weber, *Myth and the History of the Hispanic Southwest: Essays by David J. Weber* (Albuquerque: University of New Mexico Press, 1988), 1–17.

57. Most sources give the birthplace of Estavánico as Asamor, in the Berber country of North Africa. The copy of the manuscript in the Österreichische Nationalbibliothek has it this way: "estebanico es negro alarabe natural de çamora." Bibl. Pal. Vind., Cod. 5620. Zamora, of course, is in Spain. Regardless, as Donald Cutter indicates, "the invention that he was Negro rests on poor translation." See his introduction to the reprint of George Parker Winship's classic work, *The Journey of Coronado, 1540–1542* (Golden, Col.: Fulcrum, 1990), xxiii.

58. David Weber discusses the possibility that Fray Marcos de Niza did not enter present Arizona or New Mexico. See his essay, "Fray Marcos de Niza and the Historians," *Myth and the History of the Hispanic Southwest,* 19–32. For a review of the myth of the Seven Cities, see Stephen Clissold, *The Seven Cities of Cíbola* (London, Eyre and Spottiswoode, [1961]), 24–26.

59. For a brief résumé of these expeditions, see Elizabeth A. H. John, *Storms Brewed in Other Men's Worlds: The Confrontation of Indians, Spanish, and French in the Southwest, 1540–1795* (Lincoln: University of Nebraska Press, 1975), 13–23.

60. "Tierra q enbio a descubrir Don Antonio de Mendoza." The same legend appears on the Madrid, Vienna, and Stockholm maps.

61. E. W. Dahlgran cites other data to show that the Stockholm map does not depict "any discovery later than 1539." *Map of the World by Alonzo de Santa Cruz,* 27.

62. K. I. 99.416, Kartensammlung und Globenmuseum, Österreichische Nationalbibliothek, Vienna.

63. The text reads: "la florida por aqui fue cabeça de vaca."

64. For a comparison of the Gutiérrez and Cabot maps and a discussion of the various text sources, see Kelsey, "The Planispheres of Sebastian Cabot and Sancho Gutiérrez," *Terrae Incognitae* 19 (1987): 41–58.

65. Andreas Homem, "Universa ac navigabilis totius terrarum orbis descriptio," Res. Ge. CC. 2719. Bibliothèque Nationale, Paris.

66. The matter is explained at greater length in Kelsey, *Juan Rodríguez Cabrillo*, 115, 147, 220–21.

67. See the account by Pedro de Castañeda, edited by Frederick W. Hodge, in *Spanish Explorers in the Southern United States, 1528–1543* (New York: Charles Scribner's Sons, 1907), 300.

68. Harry E. Kelsey, "Ruy López de Villalobos and the Route to the Philippines," *Terrae Incognitae* 17 (1985):29–45; and "Finding the Way Home: Spanish Exploration of the Round-Trip Route across the Pacific Ocean," *Western Historical Quarterly* 17 (April 1986):145–64.

69. The Diego Gutiérrez map is "Americae sive quarte orbis partis nova et exactissima descriptio," British Library, *69810. (18.). A copy from the Library of Congress was reproduced by Walter W. Ristow, *A la Carte: Selected Papers on Maps and Atlases* (Washington, D.C.: Library of Congress, 1972), 38–42.

70. Biblioteca Apostolica Vaticana, Urb. Lat. 283. Although the atlas can be dated 1562, the North American map is based on information no later than 1539 or 1540.

71. The Gómara-Agnese view was proposed by Wagner in his *Cartography of the Northwest Coast*, 28, 45. Similar views are found in Carl I. Wheat, *Mapping the Transmississippi West, 1540–1861*, vol. 1: *The Spanish Entrada to the Louisiana Purchase, 1540–1804* (San Francisco: Institute for Historical Geography, 1957), 21–22. See also W. P. Cumming, David B. Quinn, and R. A. Skelton, *The Discovery of North America* (London: Elek Books, 1971), 131.

72. Eugene Lyon, *The Enterprise of Florida: Pedro Menéndez de Avilés and the Spanish Conquest of 1565–1568* (Gainesville: University Presses of Florida, 1974), 115, 156–57, 186, 204, map following p. 255. López de Velasco, *Geografía*, 82–88.

73. While the first label is Latin and the second Spanish, this appears to be a little bit of both, ending with the phrase a *54 grandos*. The map is in the Archivo Histórico Nacional, Madrid. There is a fairly good reproduction in Cumming, *Discovery of North America*, 173.

74. López de Velasco, *Geografía*, 82–88. The López de Velasco map of ca. 1574 is in the John Carter Brown Library, Providence, Rhode Island. Bleed-through of the ink makes the Florida detail very fuzzy. This renewed interest is also reflected in a brief summary of Florida exploration drawn up about 1568. "Relaçion q da Ju° de Velasco cosmografo mayor de su magᵗ de lo suçedido en el descubrimiento de la florida desde el año de 14 hasta el de 65," AGI, Patronato 19, ramo 23.

75. Lowery dated this map at 1595–1600 and thought it might have been drawn to accompany a report of Juan de Posada. See Lowery, *Spanish Settlements*, 464–66; tracing of the map opp. p. 286. Cumming, *The Southeast in Early Maps*, 67, accepted this date. Pedro Torres Lanzas said the map was possibly seventeenth century; see his *Relación descriptiva de los mapas, planos, & [sic], de México y Floridas existentes en el Archivo General de Indias*, 2 vols. (Seville: Imprenta de El Mercantil, 1900), 1:19–20.

76. Reproduced in several works, the best copy of the original manuscript is found in the collection of documents gathered by George P. Hammond and Agapito Rey, *The Rediscovery of New Mexico, 1500–1594* (Albuquerque: University of New Mexico Press, 1966), frontispiece. The original map is in the AGI, Mapas y planos, Mexico 6.

Plate 2.2. Map of Tepetlaoztoc from the Codex Kingsborough. By permission of the British Library, London.

92

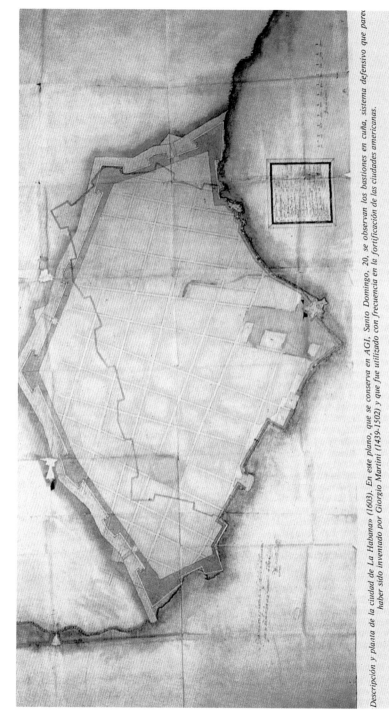

Descripción y planta de la ciudad de La Habana» (1603). En este plano, que se conserva en AGI, Santo Domingo, 20, se observan los bastiones en cuña, sistema defensivo que pare[ce] haber sido inventado por Giorgio Martini (1439-1502) y que fue utilizado con frecuencia en la fortificación de las ciudades americanas.

Plate 2.7. Cristóbal de Rojas, "Plan of Havana, Cuba, 1603." By permission of the Ministerio de Educación y Cultura, Archivo General de Indias, Seville.

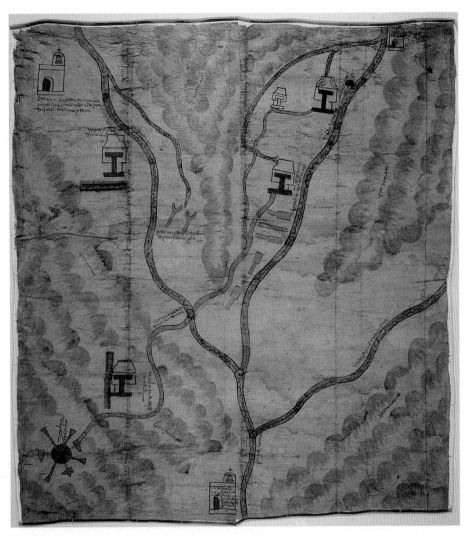

Plate 2.11. "Map of Temascaltepec." Photo courtesy of the Edward E. Ayer Collection, The Newberry Library, Chicago.

94

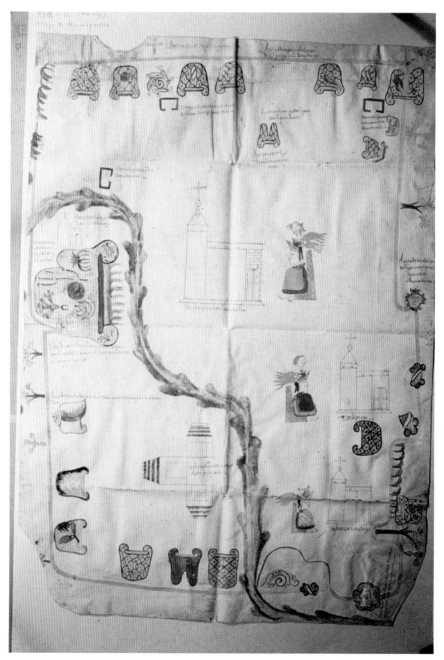

Plate 2.12. Pintura from the Relación geográphicas de Atengo, 1579. Courtesy of the Nettie Lee Benson Latin American Collection, The University of Texas at Austin, Austin, Texas.

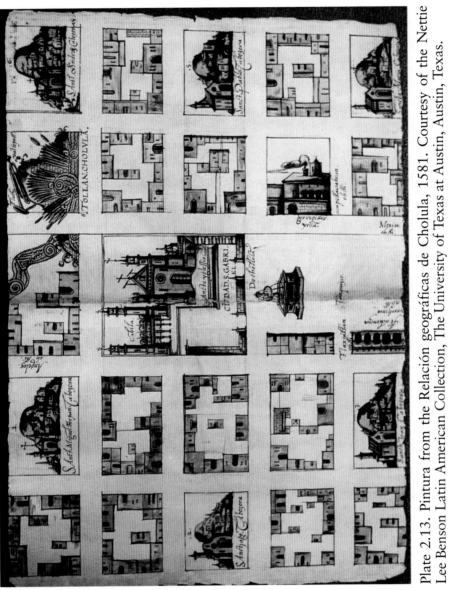

Plate 2.13. Pintura from the Relación geográficas de Cholula, 1581. Courtesy of the Nettie Lee Benson Latin American Collection, The University of Texas at Austin, Austin, Texas.

Plate 2.14. Pintura Culhuacan from the Relación geográficas de Mexicaltingo, 1580. Courtesy of the Nettie Lee Benson Latin American Collection,
The University of Texas at Austin, Austin, Texas.

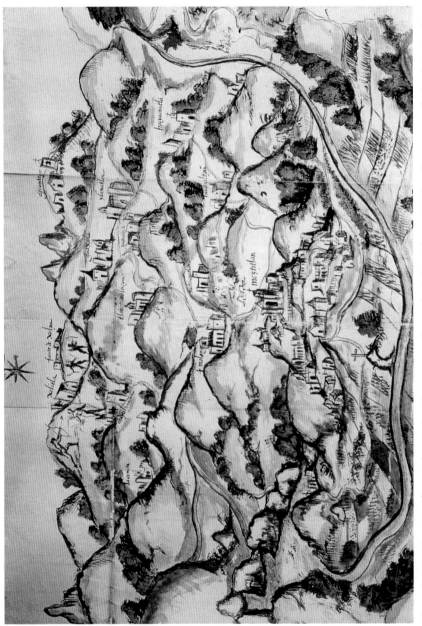

Plate 2.15. Pintura from the Relación geográficas de Meztitlan, 1579. Courtesy of the Nettie Lee Benson Latin American Collection, The University of Texas at Austin, Austin, Texas.

98

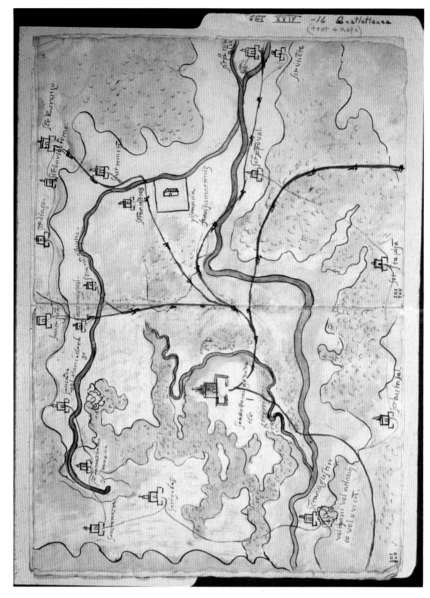

Plate 2.16. Pintura from the Relación geográficas de Quautlatlaca, 1579. Courtesy of the Nettie Lee Benson Latin American Collection, The University of Texas at Austin, Austin, Texas.

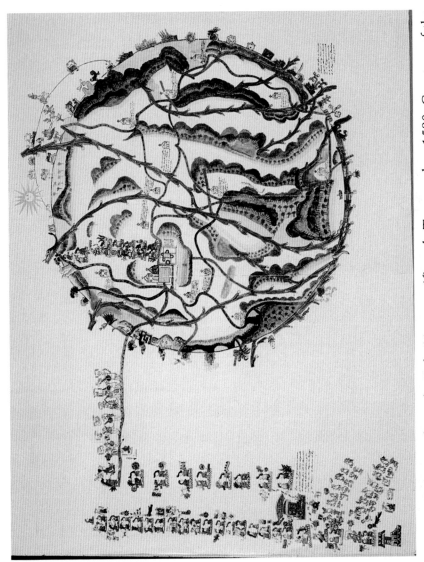

Plate 2.17. Pintura from the Relación geográficas de Teozacoalco, 1580. Courtesy of the Nettie Lee Benson Latin American Collection, The University of Texas at Austin, Austin, Texas.

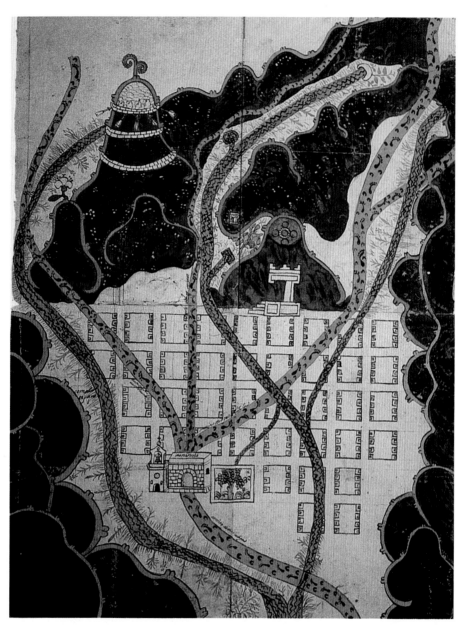

Plate 2.18. Pintura from the Relación geográficas de Texúpa, 1579. Courtesy of the Real Academia de la Historia, Madrid.

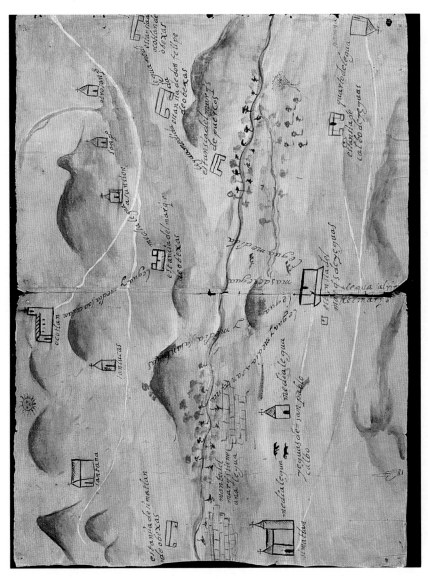

Plate 2.19. Bernave Sarmiento de Vera, "Map of Ocotlan and Simitlan (Oaxaca), Mexico, 1534." Courtesy of the Archivo General de la Nación, Mexico City.

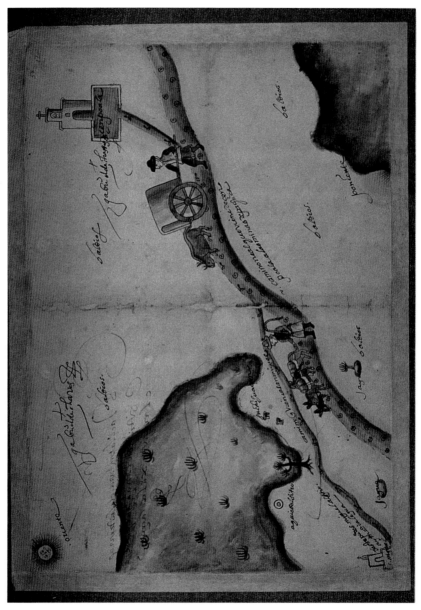

Plate 2.21. Gabriel de Chaves, "Map of Zenpoala, San Miguel, and Suchiguacan (Hidalgo), Mexico, 1589." Courtesy of the Archivo General de la Nación, Mexico City.

Plate 3.14. Detail from the Diego Gutiérrez map of 1562, which was based on Spanish maps drawn before 1554. (#69810.18.) By permission of The British Library, London.

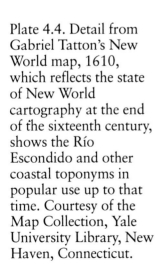

Plate 4.4. Detail from Gabriel Tatton's New World map, 1610, which reflects the state of New World cartography at the end of the sixteenth century, shows the Río Escondido and other coastal toponyms in popular use up to that time. Courtesy of the Map Collection, Yale University Library, New Haven, Connecticut.

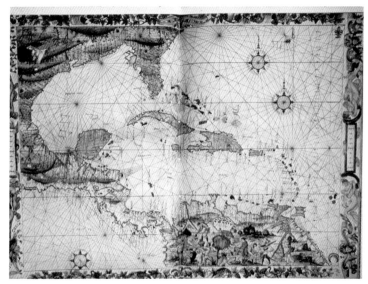

Plate 4.10. Chart of the Gulf of Mexico and the Caribbean, exemplifying the proliferation of place-names and the profuse illustration that mark many of the early printed maps; from an anonymous atlas, ca. 1540. (Ms.129.A.24, fos.23v-24r.) Courtesy of The Hague, Koninklijke Bibliotheek, Netherlands.

Plate 4.18. Abraham Ortelius, *Americae Sive Novi Orbis, Nova Descriptio* (1570), gives recognizable form to Greater North America on the basis of information provided by the sixteenth-century voyages and entradas. Courtesy of the Special Collections Division, The University of Texas at Arlington Libraries, Arlington, Texas.

Plate 5.5. Heinrich Scherer, *Provinciae Borealis Americae non ita Pridem Detecitae avt Magis ab Evropaeis Excvitae* (1720). Courtesy of the Cartographic Collections of Mrs. Jenkins Garrett, Special Collections Division, The University of Texas at Arlington Libraries, Arlington, Texas.

Plate 5.7. Didier Robert de Vaugondy, *Carte de la Californie et des Pays Nord-ouest separes de l'Asie par le détroit de Anian, extraite de deux publices au commencement du 17 Siècle par le S. Robert de Vaugondy Geog. ord. du Roi du feu Roi de Pologne Duc de Lorraine et de Bar et de l'Academie royale des Sciences et Belles-lettres de Nanci, et Censeur royal* (Paris, 1772). Courtesy of Dennis and Judy Reinhartz, Arlington, Texas.

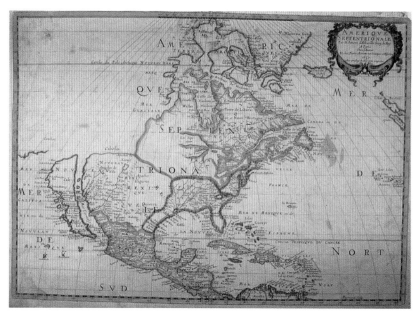

Plate 5.9. Nicolas Sanson d'Abbeville, *Amerique Septentrionale* . . . (Paris, 1650). Courtesy of the Cartographic Collections of Mrs. Jenkins Garrett, Special Collections Division, The University of Texas at Arlington Libraries, Arlington, Texas.

Plate 5.10. Sanson, detail.

IV. Coastal Exploration and Mapping

A Concomitant of the Entradas

Robert S. Weddle

Given the store of geographic knowledge available today, it is difficult to visualize the problems that confronted the first European explorers as they contemplated a trackless wilderness without guideposts of any kind. Imagine, if you can, finding yourself on a foreign shore with neither road signs nor roads; neither maps nor guidebooks; and no one to give directions except by hand gestures that are ambiguous at best. Suppose that you—equipped with only a small sailing craft and primitive navigational instruments—are obliged not only to understand this strange land but also to interpret it for others. Where would you begin?

In all likelihood, you would first try to establish the size and shape of the landmass by tracing its coastline. You would probably sail around it, making a sketch to convey its shape graphically. This is exactly what the early Spanish explorers did as they sought to comprehend the North American continent. Coastal reconnaissance preceded, then accompanied, the entradas. It was the pilots and navigators who began the mapping of the new discoveries, the process by which the Old World was given its concept of the New.

Following discovery of the Gulf of Mexico in 1508 and Juan Ponce de León's Florida discovery in 1513, three voyages were made along the southern gulf coast. They extended up the western shore as far as Cabo Rojo, fifty-odd miles south of Tampico. The third of these voyages, focusing on the wealth of the Aztec empire, was that of Hernán Cortés in 1519. The northern gulf coast, from Cabo Rojo

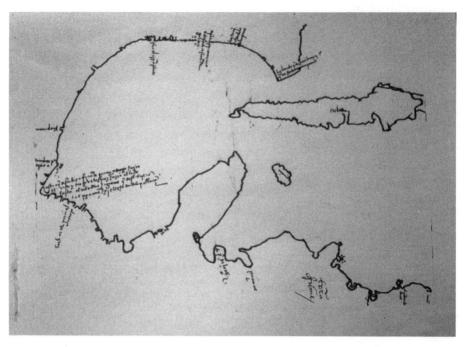

Plate 4.1. The map sketch that originated with the Álvarez de Pineda voyage, "Traza de las costas de Tierra Firme y de las Tierras Nuevas." Courtesy of the Ministerio de Educación y Cultura, Archivo General de Indias, Seville.

to Ponce de León's Florida landing place, was still unexplored. Into this void came Francisco de Garay, governor of Jamaica, who was pressed by his creditors and in desperate need of a windfall to shore up his flagging fortunes.[1]

As Cortés left Cuba, Garay armed and outfitted four ships and put them under the command of Alonso Álvarez de Pineda, a name known to us only from Bernal Díaz del Castillo, the eyewitness historian of the Mexican Conquest.[2] Pineda bridged the gap between Ponce de León's Florida landing and Cortés's beachhead on the Veracruz coast. He also proved that Florida was not an island as Ponce de León had supposed. A rudimentary sketch known as the Pineda map (plate 4.1), which the expedition's pilots presented to the Spanish Crown, revealed that no strait linked the gulf and the Pacific

Ocean.[3] The map shows the entire Gulf of Mexico. It was the very first to do so.

On the north and west, only two rivers are named: the Río del Espíritu Santo and the Río Pánuco. The Espíritu Santo is generally taken to be the Mississippi, and efforts to prove that it meant something else so far have been less than convincing.

From Garay's patent for settling this region, we know that Álvarez de Pineda had described it as peaceful, healthful, and fruitful. It was given the name Amichel. There were, according to the patent, rivers in which gold was found and natives who wore gold ornaments in nostrils and earlobes. Some of the natives, it is said, were giants almost eight feet tall; others, short people of hardly more than four feet.[4] Such descriptions soon found expression on European maps.

Juan Vespucci, for example, introduces on his 1526 map the name Río del Oro, or River of Gold (plate 4.2), on the northern gulf shore. This name—however fanciful it might have been—reflected Álvarez de Pineda's claim of gold-bearing rivers and Indians wearing gold jewelry.

The Río de los Gigantes, or Giants' River, was brought forth on two 1529 world maps by Diego Ribero (plate 4.3), Spain's royal cosmographer in the Casa de Contratación. The Casa was the agency in Seville that governed Spain's overseas commerce and collected geographic data. Ribero therefore had access to explorers' reports on the New World. The name Río de los Gigantes seems to refer to Álvarez de Pineda's eight-foot Indians—perhaps the Karankawans of the Texas coast, who were often remarked on for their great size.

The Río Escondido (Hidden River) made its appearance on an unsigned Spanish map dated 1527, thought also to have been Ribero's work.[5] It is most often shown in the Texas coastal bend, where the Nueces River empties into Corpus Christi Bay (plate 4.4, page 103). The Nueces mouth is so well concealed behind barrier islands that it took Spanish explorers 220 years to identify it and connect it with the stream that rises on the Edwards Plateau. Until 1747 the Nueces was believed tributary to the Rio Grande.[6] Who but Álvarez de Pineda might have provided information on it by 1527?

Plate 4.2. Detail from Juan Vespucci's planisphere, 1526. Courtesy of the Hispanic Society of America, New York.

Plate 4.3. Detail from Diego Ribero's world map of 1529, in the Vatican. (Borgiano 3.) Photo courtesy of the Biblioteca Vaticana, Rome.

The 1529 Ribero Weimar map, which is similar but not identical to the map in the Vatican (plate 4.3), contains some interesting notations on the character of the Texas gulf coast.[7] Between the Río del Oro and the Río Escondido appear the words *playa baxa* and *anegadizo*, describing a low, level beach subject to flooding (plate 4.5). South of the Escondido, in the Padre Island vicinity, Ribero notes *malabrigo*, indicating an exposed anchorage—a lee shore on which ships might come to grief. A quarter century later, in 1554, three Spanish merchant vessels found their graves there, as countless others have since (plate 4.6).[8] In sum, data emanating from cosmographers in the Casa de Contratación in the late 1520s suggest that Álvarez de Pineda's voyage yielded more knowledge of the gulf coasts than is generally recognized.

The first map specifically of the Gulf of Mexico to be printed appeared with a 1524 edition of Cortés's Second Letter to the Crown (plate 4.7). It is therefore known as "the Cortés map," even though

Plate 4.5. The *playa baxa* and *anegadizo* shown on the Ribero Weimer map brings to mind the Texas coast, between San Antonio and Aransas bays, wintering ground of the endangered whooping crane. Photo by Robert S. Weddle.

Plate 4.6. Ribero's description of a coast lacking shelter for ships (*malabrigo*) still holds in the twentieth century. This hulk of a wooden vessel was uncovered by wave action on Padre Island National Seashore, 1977. Photo by Robert S. Weddle.

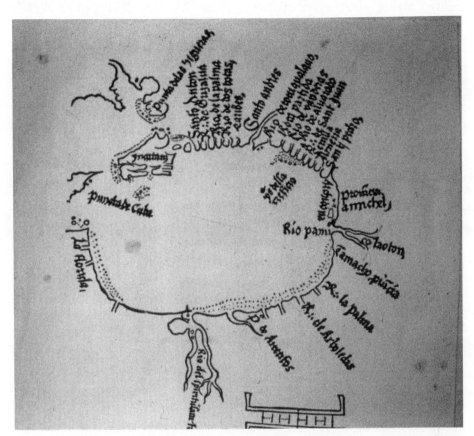

Plate 4.7. The first printed map of the Gulf of Mexico, published with Hernán Cortés's Second Letter to the Spanish Crown in 1524. The map is oriented with south at the top. Courtesy of the Ministerio de Educación y Cultura, Archivo General de Indias, Seville.

we may be fairly certain that Cortés was not the author. His authorship seemingly is refuted by his inclusion of the name Provincia de Amichel, which was Garay's territory, while omitting his own Villa Rica de la Vera Cruz.[9]

One interesting feature of the map is its representation, with a profusion of dots, of the shoals along the coast west of the Mississippi. Like the Álvarez de Pineda sketch, the map shows both the Río Pánuco and the Río del Espíritu Santo. The bay at the mouth of the latter is somewhat larger than Álvarez de Pineda's and has a different configuration. Two river names not on Álvarez de Pineda's sketch have been added—Río de Arboledas (River of Woodlands) and Río de las Palmas (River of Palms). The Río de las Palmas has often been confused with the Rio Grande. It was named by Garay in 1523, when he was on his way to Pánuco to renew the colony founded previously by Álvarez de Pineda, who had been slain in a Huastec uprising.[10] The Río de las Palmas was not the Rio Grande but the Soto la Marina River, entering the gulf about 150 miles farther south, at the small fishing village of La Pesca, Tamaulipas (plates 4.8, 4.9). The Río Bravo, as the Rio Grande is called in Mexico, was slow to appear on maps and took even longer to be given its recognizable form. Since the Río de las Palmas often was shown as the first river south of the Río Escondido, it was natural to mistake it for the Rio Grande.[11]

Publication of the "Cortés map" inspired other efforts, mostly aimed at satisfying the popular demand. They showed nothing more than the general coastal outline, with names for rivers taken from any source at hand. Ribero's two 1529 world maps, being fair representations of the Spanish *padrón real*, or master chart, kept in the Casa de Contratación, were prototypes. Their toponyms were often repeated, though sometimes shifted about indiscriminately. The names also tended to be corrupted, a natural result of frequent transcription and often of the copyist's lack of familiarity with the original language and script. Each successive map seems to have more place-names than its predecessor, pointing not so much to expansion of geographic knowledge as to mapmakers' attempts to use all the designations available.[12] Those competing to satisfy the European demand were shameless plagiarists (plate 4.10, page 104).

Configurations, tending to follow a set pattern, were copied too, although with an occasional imaginative touch. Álvarez de Pineda's bay—called Bahía del Espíritu Santo or Mar Pequeño—most often was given the configuration from the "Cortés map," which was more readily accessible than the Álvarez de Pineda sketch. The bay, enlarged and altered in different ways, endured as a map feature until late in the seventeenth century. No one ventured to detail the river

Plate 4.8. The mouth of the Río de las Palmas (Soto la Marina, often confused with the Rio Grande) at La Pesca, Tamaulipas. Photo by Robert S. Weddle.

Plate 4.9. The Soto la Marina River several miles above its mouth, where it is joined by a southern tributary still known as Las Palmas. Photo by Robert S. Weddle.

courses or scarcely any other significant inland features until what is known as the "De Soto map" appeared. This map was one of two found among the papers of the royal cosmographer Alonso de Santa Cruz on his death in 1572.[13] The other was Santa Cruz's general map of the Caribbean Sea, the Gulf of Mexico, and the east coast of North America. Although it has been dated as early as 1536, it has the Médanos de Madalena, representing the Padre Island dunes. That name, bestowed by salvagers of the three lost ships mentioned previously, did not emerge until 1554.

The two Santa Cruz maps are different enough to raise doubts of their common authorship. Note, for example, the different shape given the bay at the mouth of the Mississippi, with four rivers flowing into it. The "Soto Map," in contrast, follows the Cortés rendering (plate 4.11).

The Soto map, of course, gets its name from the expedition of Hernando de Soto, which provided much of its information. It is often dated soon after the entrada ended, about 1544, but no one really knows, since it did not come to light until 1572. In any case, it is misleading to call it the Soto map. It draws from several other explorers, including Ponce de León and Lucas Vázquez de Ayllón in the east and Alvar Núñez Cabeza de Vaca and Francisco Vázquez de Coronado in the southwest.

The map's coastal outline, however, probably did come from Soto's men; specifically, from Juan de Añasco. Añasco was the expedition's comptroller and principal pathfinder who charted the course that enabled the survivors to reach Pánuco by sea. It was he also who had reconnoitered the Florida landing place before Soto's main fleet set sail from Cuba and who conducted the fleet from the first landing site to Apalachee Bay. For charting the course from the Mississippi to Pánuco, Añasco repaired the astrolabe burned in the fire at Mauvila; he manufactured a cross-staff from a ruler and constructed a sea chart on a piece of deerskin. He still carried a mariner's clock that he had brought from Spain and kept safely through all the journey's trials.[14]

Reaching Matagorda Bay, Soto's men sailed up it a short distance but could not see its end. Two days later they entered another bay,

Plate 4.11. The "De Soto map" by Alonso de Santa Cruz. (Mapas y planos, Mexico 1.) Courtesy of the Ministerio de Educación y Cultura, Archivo General de Indias, Seville.

probably the Aransas—Corpus Christi bay complex. At some point along the shore they found huge blobs of tar (plate 4.12), such as still wash up on Padre Island National Seashore from a natural source. They used the substance to seal the bottoms of their leaky boats.[15] Thus they were able to reach Pánuco, long after they had been given up for dead.

Yet the Santa Cruz–Soto map (plate 4.11) seems to represent a running account of New World explorations rather than a single expedition. It contains data that neither Añasco nor others of Soto's army could have provided. Near the mouth of the Río Grande, which Santa Cruz calls Río Solo, for example, the cosmographer shows mountains and notes that they contain silver. Such information probably came from Cabeza de Vaca.

The Pánfilo de Narváez expedition, of which Cabeza de Vaca was a part, became scattered along the Texas coast from Galveston

Plate 4.12. Soto's survivors, sailing along the coast toward Pánuco, availed themselves of tar that had washed up on Texas beaches to caulk their leaky vessels. The substance still washes up on Padre National Seashore from natural seeps around the Gulf of Mexico. This specimen was found in 1977. Photo by Robert S. Weddle.

Bay to the Rio Grande in 1528, while trying to reach Pánuco. Many of the expeditionists, including Narváez himself, perished in the Matagorda Bay vicinity, leaving only Cabeza de Vaca and three companions. After escaping their Indian captors near the coastal bend late in 1534, the four survivors traveled southwest until they crossed a river described as being as wide as the Guadalquivir at Seville—the Rio Grande—and soon saw mountains extending "from the direction of the North Sea." The "North Sea" in this context means the Gulf of Mexico. The mountains extending from it comprise the Sierra Madre Oriental, first encountered south of the lower Rio Grande near Cerralvo, Nuevo León—too far inland to have been seen by Soto's men sailing along the coast. But Cabeza de Vaca, walking west across northern Mexico, surely saw them.[16]

Another mapmaker's note, on the Rio Grande's left bank some distance above the mouth, declares that "from Quivira to this point there are great herds of cattle." The "cattle," of course, were buffalo, which were seldom seen in large numbers below the Rio Grande. The reference to Quivira suggests a link to the Coronado expedition through the Portuguese soldier and gardener Andrés de Campo. Campo remained on the Kansas plains with Fray Juan Padilla when Coronado's army withdrew. Following Padilla's death, he fled south with two Indian companions. Some years after the Soto men had gone on to Mexico City, he reached Pánuco with the first news of the friar's martyrdom.[17]

The Santa Cruz–Soto map, as T. H. Lewis has put it, revealed "how little was known of the Gulf coast and its interior connections." Lewis says it "supplies the best information of that day regarding the towns and rivers of the interior." Of some sixty Indian towns shown, fourteen are identifiable with those named in the three primary accounts of Soto's march through the South.[18] Yet the river courses on the whole are far from accurate. The Mississippi, or Espíritu Santo, which the expeditionists had sailed on for seventeen days, is shown, like one of the two branches given it on the "Cortés Map," flowing straight south into a bay that has the Cortés configuration. The Red River is not connected to it. There is a bare semblance of accuracy to some of the other rivers west of the Mississippi that were seen on the march led by Luis de Moscoso into eastern Texas and again from the gulf. But the map is badly askew from having the Río del Espíritu Santo placed so far west. Some of the information on both Texas Indian villages and river courses may have come from Cabeza de Vaca, who traded among the eastern Texas natives for nearly three years before proceeding down the coast.

The Soto map had a certain appeal that influenced other mapmakers. Gerónimo de Chaves's 1584 map of "La Florida" (plate 4.13) has been termed "a simplified variant" of Santa Cruz's work and is credited with extending its influence over the ensuing forty years.[19] The Chaves map does reflect the Soto map's style and much of its content while incorporating some new coastal toponyms and altered concepts.

Plate 4.13. Gerónimo de Chaves's 1584 map, *La Florida*. Courtesy of the Cartographic Collections of Mrs. Jenkins Garrett, Special Collections Division, The University of Texas at Arlington Libraries.

Moscoso and the Soto survivors reached Mexico City late in 1543, about a year after Vázquez de Coronado had returned from the Cíbola expedition. Attendant to the planning and execution of Vázquez de Coronado's march north to seek the fabulous land reported by Cabeza de Vaca, three voyages were made along the Pacific coast from Mexico. The first was conducted on Cortés's behalf by Francisco de Ulloa. The second, sent to support Vázquez de Coronado, was led by Hernando de Alarcón. The final one, seeking news of Vázquez de Coronado on his return, was begun by Juan Rodríguez Cabrillo and completed by his chief pilot, Bartolomé Ferrelo, after Cabrillo's death. These voyages opened new vistas for European cartographers, who yet had little understanding of the Pacific coast of North America. The 1540 map of Sebastian Münster (plate 4.14) though not typical in every respect, shows some of the

Plate 4.14. Sebastian Münster's 1550 map, reflecting a concept of North America prior to the Pacific Coast voyages of 1539–41. Courtesy of the Cartographic Collections of Mrs. Jenkins Garrett, Special Collections Division, The University of Texas at Arlington Libraries.

confused ideas that lingered in the minds of mapmakers, placing Japan closer to California than the west coast of Mexico to the east.

Cortés, though stripped of his powers as governor, still claimed the right to lead the northward exploration. He had explored the west coast into the Gulf of California and, at the site of present-day La Paz on the Baja Peninsula, had founded a short-lived colony called Santa Cruz. His activities, however, were not favored by the Crown, which had long since become doubtful of his methods and suspicious of his motives. After 1530 the newly appointed royal *audiencia* (tribunal) blocked his every move; then, in 1535, Antonio de Mendoza became New Spain's first viceroy. Mendoza relished the prospect of dampening Cortés's ambitions.

Plate 4.15. Ulloa's landfall on the Sinaloa coast, near present-day Topolobampo. Photo by Robert S. Weddle.

Nevertheless, as the Cíbola expedition made its preparations, Cortés still insisted on his right to conduct the northward exploration. Failing in all overtures to Mendoza, he outfitted three ships in defiance of the viceroy. With Francisco de Ulloa in command, he sent them up the Pacific Coast, seeking the fabled Cíbola.

Ulloa, a veteran of Cortés's Pacific Coast explorations, had been in charge of the Santa Cruz colony on the Baja Peninsula. He sailed from Acapulco in July 1539 and reached La Paz Bay early in September. He then set sail across the gulf to reach the mainland near present-day Topolobampo, Sinaloa, at the mouth of the Río San Pedro y San Pablo— today's Río Fuerte (plate 4.15). Thence he sailed up the mainland coast, marking capes, river mouths, and islands never before glimpsed by Europeans, until he reached the mouth of the Colorado River. Prevented by shoals from entering the river, he descended the peninsula, doubled Cabo San Lucas, and ran north along the outer coast almost to latitude 29°. In the last of several battles with Indians, Ulloa was wounded and spent from January to April at Isla Cedros. The turning point, eighteen leagues beyond, was called Cabo del Engaño, or False Cape.[20]

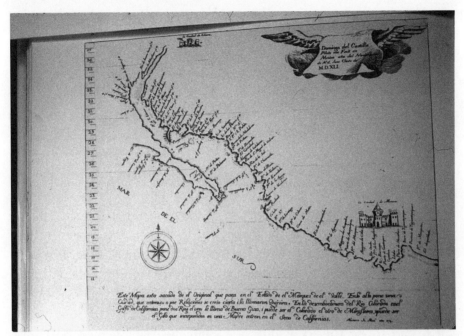

Plate 4.16. Domingo del Castillo's map sketch reflecting the voyages of both Ulloa and Alarcón. In *Historia de Nueva España, escrita por su esclarecida conquistador Hernán Cortés,* by Francisco Antonio Lorenzana (Mexico City: Imprenta del Supremo Gobierno, 1770). Courtesy of the DeGolyer Library, Southern Methodist University, Dallas.

Cortes's biographer, Francisco López de Gómara, makes light of Ulloa's voyage because it accomplished nothing to benefit Cortés.[21] Yet it traced some two thousand miles of coastline, discovered the mouth of the Colorado River, and provided evidence that California was not an island. The map of this part of the continent, in consequence, was reshaped to include the Vermilion Sea and the long peninsula that enclosed it on the west. Ulloa's report describes the making of a map by his pilots, but the map has been lost. Fortunately, Domingo del Castillo, who was on this voyage, later sailed as pilot and mapmaker with Alarcón and drew a map that encompasses both voyages (plate 4.16).[22]

Cortés, meanwhile, was out of the picture. Locked in a power struggle with Mendoza, he went to Spain in 1540 to lay his grievances before the Crown. He was not permitted to return.

Alarcón, carrying supplies to Vázquez de Coronado's army, sailed from Acapulco on March 9, 1540, two months after Vázquez de Coronado marched north from Compostela. Entering the gulf, his small fleet ran northwest along the mainland shore, marking bays not noted by Ulloa. On August 26 the ships hove to at the shoals that marked Ulloa's turning point. Alarcón sent his pilots, Nicolás Zamorano and Castillo, in a launch to sound a passage. The ships, attempting to follow, ran aground. They lay immobile and helpless until the "miracle" of a rising tide floated them free. Past this barrier, as Alarcón tells it, "we found a mighty river with so furious a current that we could scarcely sail against it." Anchored in its mouth, he could proclaim himself the first explorer to enter the Colorado River of the West. He named it Buena Guía, or Unfailing Guide, from the motto on Mendoza's coat of arms. Some maps would label it Río de Alarcón; others, Río de Tiguex.[23]

Alarcón ascended the river with twenty men and two boats, which had to be towed against the swift current by men on shore. Indian archers in hostile stance often forced the boatmen to withdraw to midstream. Gradually, gifts won them over. These natives, of whom Alarcón provides the first description, were the Cócopa, Quícama, and Kohuana of Yuman linguistic stock.[24]

From the Indians Alarcón obtained news of Vázquez de Coronado's movements but was never able to link up with the army. In late September 1540 he erected a cross and left on it a message for any of Vázquez de Coronado's men who might come looking for him. The message was found two months later by Melchior Díaz, fifteen leagues above the mouth of the Colorado—somewhat less than Alarcón's exaggerated claim. Castillo's map, failing to show the Yuma bend, indicates that the ascent ended short of the Gila River mouth.

While Alarcón was returning, Pedro de Alvarado came from Guatemala with his own fleet to take part in northern exploration and garnered a partnership in the enterprise with Mendoza. After Alvarado had lost his life in the Mixtón War, Mendoza owned his entire fleet. He assigned three of the ships to Cabrillo, an Alvarado associate, and sent him up the coast to seek news of Vázquez de

Plate 4.17. This map of the southern part of North America, which appeared in a portolan atlas in 1557, is attributed to Battista Agnese. Reflecting Cabrillo's toponyms, it shows the Sierra Nevada but places Quivira and Tigeux much too far west. Photo courtesy of the Edward E. Ayer Collection, The Newberry Library, Chicago.

Coronado. He, however, had already reached Culiacán on his way back to Mexico City. Cabrillo sailed from Navidad on June 27, 1542, to ascend the outer shore of the peninsula and the mainland coast to San Diego Bay. Continuing north, he discovered Santa Barbara Channel and the Channel Islands and took possession of the mainland for Spain. After reaching a point beyond San Francisco Bay, Cabrillo withdrew to Catalina Island for the winter. He died there on January 3, 1543. The chief pilot, Ferrelo, succeeded to command. Ferrelo voyaged north as far as Oregon and returned to Navidad the following April.[25] The 1557 map of Battista Agnese reflects the Cabrillo-Ferrelo discoveries in its toponyms (plate 4.17). One of these features is the Sierra Nevada, which got its name from the Cabrillo expedition.

The voyages that were ancillary to Vázquez de Coronado's entrada had explored the entire coast of the Californias, including both sides of the Sea of Cortés, or the Vermilion Sea—afterward called the Gulf of California. As the efforts of Álvarez de Pineda, Narváez, and Soto were crucial to expanding commerce between Spain and "the Indies," the Pacific Coast voyages aided the soon-to-be Far East trade. Ships sailing east across the Pacific had to steer far to the north to find favorable wind and current. Their first landfall on the California coast was above latitude 40°. Thence, the ships followed the coast southward to Acapulco, within sight of land most of the way.[26]

In sum, the sixteenth-century coastal voyages and the crude maps they contributed were not only a giant step toward defining the continental outline but also a necessary concomitant of the entradas. Within five years after Álvarez de Pineda's voyage—and within a year after publication of the so-called Cortés map—European cartographers were at work revising their renderings of eastern North America to include the Gulf of Mexico. In similar fashion the voyages of Ulloa, Alarcón, and Cabrillo opened a new frontier for mapmakers, enabling them to portray the continent to its far limits (plate 4.18, page 104). In some cases, however, the information traveled slowly, or fashion overcame established fact. A century later it became fashionable to depict California as an island, an anomaly that finds a ready market among present-day collectors. One dealer's recent catalog lists nine maps, dated from 1686 to 1761, showing an insular California (plate 4.19).[27]

The precise route by which data found their way from the explorers' logbooks and sketches to the printed maps that gave Europeans their concept of the New World is not always easily discernible. Spain, as the discovering nation, regarded its geographic data and maps of new territories as secret. Hence there are few surviving Spanish general maps that reflect the American discoveries: it was left to mapmakers of other nations to shape Europeans' views of New World geography. In doing so, they often perpetuated inaccurate and confused information, with place-names badly rendered

Plate 4.19. Herman Moll's 1720 map of North America, "According to ye Newest and most Exact observations," is one of many of this period showing California as an island—a concept disproved by explorations of the 1540s. Courtesy of the Special Collections Division, The University of Texas at Arlington Libraries.

and misapplied. But, for accuracy, the mapmakers—Italian, German, Dutch, and French—were largely dependent on the early Spanish voyages and entradas and information that flowed, by whatever means, from the database in the Casa de Contratación in Seville.

Geographic knowledge from the sixteenth-century entradas was restricted by the very nature of their experience. The struggle to survive often transcended the concern for enlightenment. For this reason Soto's survivors failed to define the course of the Mississippi and how it entered the gulf. It was a costly omission; had the waterway been recognized as the key to the continent, Spain might have possessed it before the French did. The oversight was costly for the French, too: had Sieur de La Salle been able to reconcile his own observations while descending the Mississippi in 1682 with the meager information from Soto's march around 1540, he might never have landed in Texas and his colony would have been spared its tragic end.[28]

Despite such failures, one may contemplate with sheer amazement the sixteenth-century maps pertaining to the American Southwest: so much was accomplished during the first hundred years. The cartographic strides of the sixteenth century are summed up by Tatton's map (plate 4.4, page 103), which was crafted at the century's very end. Its ornate quality, its tentative coastal outline, its corruption of place-names and hypothetical river courses are representative of the state of knowledge at that point and of how concepts of the New World were presented in Europe. Great blank spaces and distortions still existed on maps of the Southwest and its two coasts; there in lay the challenge of the coming centuries.

NOTES

1. Concerning Garay's motivation, see Archivo Protocolos de Sevilla (APS), 1508–14, oficios 1, 14; Robert S. Weddle, *Spanish Sea: The Gulf of Mexico in North American Discovery, 1500–1685* (College Station: Texas A&M University Press, 1985), 97, 106.

2. Bernal Díaz del Castillo, *Historia verdadera de la conquista de la Nueva España* (Mexico City: Editorial Porrúa, 1955), 2:104.

3. "Real cédula dando facultad a Francisco de Garay para poblar la provincia de Amichel," in Martín Fernández de Navarrete, *Colección de los viages y descubrimientos que hicieron por mar los españoles* (Reprint Buenos Aires: Editorial Guarania, 1945), 3;147–53.

4. Ibid.

5. Henry G. Taliaferro, "Introduction: Early Cartography of the Texas Coast," in *Cartographic Sources in the Rosenberg Library*, edited by Jane A. Kenamore and Uli Haller (College Station: Texas A&M University Press, 1988), 6.

6. José de Escandón to the viceroy, October 28, 1747, Archivo General de la Nación, Mexico (AGN), Provincias Internas 179, pt. 1, transcript, Barker Texas History Center, University of Texas at Austin (BTHC), 2Q212.

7. Detail of the Ribero Weimar map in Jean Delanglez, *El Rio del Espíritu Santo: An Essay on the Cartography of the Gulf Coast and the Adjacent Territory during the Sixteenth and Seventeenth Centuries* (New York: United States Catholic Historical Society, 1945), pl. 2.

8. Concerning the 1554 shipwrecks, see Robert S. Weddle, "History," in J. Barto Arnold III and Robert S. Weddle, *The Nautical Archeology of Padre Island: The Spanish Shipwrecks of 1554* (New York: Academic Press, 1978).

9. For a discussion of the "Cortés map," see Weddle, *Spanish Sea*, 159–60.

10. Pedro Mártir de Angleriá (Peter Martyr), *Décadas del Nuevo Mundo*, translated by D. Joaquín Torres Ascensio (Buenos Aires: Editorial Bajel, 1944), 570; Díaz del Castillo, *Historia verdadera*, 2:104.

11. The distinction is clearly drawn in countless colonial documents, apart from the Peter Martyr account of the Garay expedition; e.g., those dealing with the explorations of Luis de Carvajal y de la Cueva (1572) and Alonso de León (1686). Yet the National Geographic Society map *Spain in the Americas* (February 1992) identifies the Río de las Palmas with the Río Grande. The society's chief cartographer, John F. Shupe, has revealed to the writer the source of this error (Paul Horgan, *Great River: The Rio Grande in North American History* [1954]), adding the comment, "I believe further research is needed regarding this feature." (R.S.W. to John F. Shupe, January 31, 1992; Shupe to R.S.W., March 6, 1992.)

12. Taliaferro, "Introduction," 8.

13. Juan López de Velasco (*Geografía y descripción universal de las Indias* [Madrid: Ediciones Atlas, 1971], 93), writing in the 1570s, attributes the map to Santa Cruz, saying there was no better description of La Florida or its native habitations.

14. Juan de Añasco, "Probanza," Puebla de los Ángeles, May 30, 1544, ACI, Patronato 57, no. 1, ramo 3.

15. "The Gentleman of Elvas," in *Narratives of De Soto in the Conquest of Florida*, translated by Buckingham Smith (Gainesville, Fla.: Palmetto Books, 1968), 189.

16. Weddle, *Spanish Sea*, 201–2; Donald E. Chipman, "In Search of Cabeza de Vaca's Route across Texas: An Historiographical Survey," *Southwestern Historical Quarterly* 91, no. 2 (October 1987): 127–48.

17. Concerning Campo, see Angelico Chavez, *Coronado's Friars* (Washington, D.C.: Academy of American Franciscan History, 1968), 67–68; and Herbert Eugene Bolton, *Coronado: Knight of Pueblo and Plains* (Albuquerque: University of New Mexico Press, 1964), 360.

18. T. H. Lewis, "The Chroniclers of the De Soto Expedition," *Publications of the Mississippi Historical Society* 7 (1903): 385–86.

19. Delanglez, *El Rio del Espíritu Santo*, 71.

20. Hubert Howe Bancroft, *History of the North Mexican States and Texas* (San Francisco: A. L. Bancroft, 1884), 1:78. Bancroft translates the name as Cape Disappointment.

21. Henry R. Wagner, *The Spanish Settlement* (Reprint New York: Arno Press, 1967), 1:104.

22. Bolton, *Coronado*, 168; Bancroft, *History of the North Mexican States and Texas*, 1:81; Justin Winsor, ed., *Narrative and Critical History of America* (Boston: Houghton Mifflin, 1886), 2:444; W. P. Cumming, R. A. Skelton, and D. B. Quinn, *The Discovery of North America* (New York: American Heritage Press, 1972), 102.

23. Bolton, *Coronado*, 155 (quote). The Tatton 1600 map (pl. 4.4) calls the river Río de Alarcón; Battista Agnese (pl. 4.18) calls it R. de Tiguex.

24. John R. Swanton, *The Indian Tribes of North America* (Washington, D.C.: Smithsonian Institution, 1952), 349, 350, 354.

25. A biography of Cabrillo is Harry E. Kelsey, *Juan Rodríguez Cabrillo* (San Marino, Calif.: Huntington Library, 1986). For the Alvarado-Cabrillo relationship and their connection with the expedition to the Spice Islands led by Ruy López de Villalobos, see Harry E. Kelsey, "Ruy López de Villalobos and the Route to the Philippines," *Terrae Incognitae* 17 (1985): 29–45. Documents related to Cabrillos' voyage up the west coast are translated in Herbert Eugene Bolton, ed., *Spanish Exploration of the Southwest, 1542–1706* (Reprint New York: Barnes and Noble, 1963), 13–39. Sources are discussed by Winsor, *Narrative and Critical History*, 2:444n; Bancroft,

History of the North Mexican States and Texas, 1:133n; and Wagner, *Spanish Southwest*, 1:187–91.

26. Kelsey, "Ruy López de Villalobos," 44–45. See also Eugene Lyon, "Track of the Manila Galleons," *National Geographic* 178, no. 3 (September 1990): 35.

27. Art Source International, *Catalog Number 22* (Boulder, Col.: Art Source International, December 1991), 2–3.

28. See Peter H. Wood, "La Salle: Discovery of a Lost Explorer," *American Historical Review* 89, no. 2 (April 1984): 294–323; Robert S. Weddle, *The French Thorn: Rival Explorers in the Spanish Sea, 1682–1762* (College Station: Texas A&M University Press, 1991), 3–40.

V. LEGADO

The Information of the Entradas Portrayed through the Early Nineteenth Century

Dennis Reinhartz

The most celebrated cosmographers have always divided the world into three parts: Europe, Asia, Africa are their names, clear and beautiful. Europe, which is the smallest of the three, whose capital is Rome, contains France, Spain and Italy, and stretches from Norway to Crete and from Germany to Sardinia. Africa, more extensive, once prided itself on the triumph and glory of Carthage, and contains Libya, Ethiopia, Egypt and the land from Numidia to Mauritania. Asia, which formerly gave obeyance to Troy, includes Media, Persia, Albania, Palestine and Judea, Scythia, Arabia and India. But, outside of these three parts, more are to be found, I do not believe, unless you subdivide them, or unless you claim to know more than the great Ptolemy. . . . Go, my friend, cure your sick brain; do not be like the alchemists, but stick to the realities and try to discover what is already known. Do not try to see an incredible world through a crack in the door, or by the light of a lantern search the teachings of maps and libraries. How would you believe that a line drawn on paper is the route of the sun . . . ? Fools, who are always seeking their own misfortune and bringing only trouble to kings!

The king of Portugal rejecting Columbus

As the above satirical lines from *The Discovery of the New World by Christopher Columbus*, a 1614(?) play by Lope de Vega, a founder of Spanish drama, alluded, in 1492 Columbus not only saw "through a crack" but also opened the "door" for Europe, Africa, and Asia to view a new world. Each of the expeditions that followed, like those led by Ponce de León in 1513, Alonso Álvarez de Pineda in 1519, and Hernán Cortés in 1519–21, gradually extended the Old World's vision and broadened its horizons.

In the North American Greater Southwest, no journeys of exploration were more revealing than the three great entradas of Pánfilo de Narváez and Alvar Núñez Cabeza de Vaca in 1527–37, Fray Marcos de Niza and Francisco Vázquez de Coronado in 1539–42, and Hernando de Soto and Luis de Moscoso in 1539–43. These ambitious, courageous, and flamboyant conquistadors (and their patrons) were motivated by various factors that colored their visions and reports about the vast domains they explored. They came out of curiosity, seeking fortune and glory for themselves, their rulers, and their God. The new lands to the north of Mexico City perhaps held yet other Aztec and Inca empires to be conquered, a swift water passage to the riches of Asia, and numerous souls in need of salvation. These three entradas particularly constitute a formative early chapter in the intellectual and cultural history of the "Columbian exchange" as well as in the multicultural history of the Greater Southwest.

While most of the major stated financial and geographic objectives of the entradas were not realized, they contributed immensely to the Old World's knowledge of the Greater Southwest. The vast and often barren lands of Cíbola and Quivira were indeed devoid of wealth like that of the Aztecs and Incas, but they were rich in diverse Amerindian peoples, from the Hopi, Zuñi and Tigua to the Pawnee and Wichita of the Great Plains. From the Colorado to the Mississippi, most of the region's important rivers were crossed and explored. Still other natural wonders—the Grand Canyon and Palo Duro Canyon as well as great herds of buffalo and the oil seeps of

East Texas—were also observed. The actual accomplishment of the entradas was simply and perhaps best stated by Pedro de Castañeda, a participant in and chronicler of Vázquez de Coronado's expedition: "Granted that they did not find the riches of which they had been told, they found a place in which to search for them and a good country to settle in, so as to go farther from there."[1] In the process, although some myths were dispelled, others remained to be transformed and perpetuated.

The imagery of North America that emerged from the entradas is interesting and significant not only because of its geographic content and misconceptions but also because of its influence on further exploration and discovery. To the north of the Spanish traverses, the continent was seen as opening up like a fan, the central ribs of which were formed by estuaries of the great Missouri-Mississippi system. The principal source of this river network was believed to be a range of high mountains (the Rockies?), related by various Amerindian attesters to be somewhere to the northwest of Quivira near the Pacific Ocean and Asia. Another chain of mountains (the Appalachians?) was seen as coming in from the east at a latitude north of Quivira. Based on this continental view, cartographers for many years incorrectly showed the Appalachians running more east to west than north to south. At its widest, the continent stretched for more than one thousand miles (still only approximately one-third of its actual size but far better than the ninefold underestimation of the Ptolemy-Columbus global vision) from the Atlantic near Iceland to the Pacific near China with a passage connecting the two oceans somewhere to the north (apparently reinforced by the discovery of the St. Lawrence River by the French explorer Jacques Cartier in 1535).[2] The northwest coast of America was held to be not-too-distantly separated from Asia by the fabled Strait of Anian. Eventually, cartographers placed Quivira, the Totonteac of the Hopis, and other lands discovered by Vázquez de Coronado on the eastern shore of this strait and even made the strait itself a northwest passage.[3]

The information revealed by the entradas reached the Old World via some of their actual participants and their writings and, perhaps more important, via the manuscript and printed maps of the period. Even by the early nineteenth century, in a still largely illiterate Europe, the growing body of graphic imagery had an especially powerful effect on the course of the discovery, exploration, and exploitation of the New World. Of real significance was the continuing impact of this imagery on the shaping of popular European perceptions and misperceptions of the Americas and especially of the Greater Southwest and West. Here, in an effort to achieve an understanding of these complex, interesting, and related processes of information transmission and concept formation, the cartographic legacy of the entradas will be explored through the analysis of a selection of popular printed maps, dating from 1600 to 1802.[4]

The Strait of Anian between North America and Asia had first appeared on maps in the 1560s, and it remained on some until the early nineteenth century, but rumors of its existence were initially associated with the voyages of Gaspar and Miguel Cortereal to explore the northern Canadian coasts for the king of Portugal in 1500–02.[5] An early-seventeenth-century map that showed clearly the presence of the strait is "Typvs Orbis Terrarvm . . ." (ca. 1600), associated with the German geographer-cartographer Matthias Quad von Kinckelbach (plates 5.1, 5.2). As indicated in the full title, it is based on the planisphere world map of 1569 by the great Gerardus Mercator.[6] This widely distributed map not only shows "El streto de Anian" off the west coast of North America but also the lands of "Anian Regnum" and Vázquez de Coronado's "Regnu Quivira," "Quivira," and "Tiguex" as well as the Hopi "Axa Tontene" right on the coast along and south of the strait. The name "America" on this map was copied from Mercator, who in turn took it from Martin Waldseemüller. Waldseemüller, being ignorant of Columbus's achievement, first used the appellation on one of his maps in 1507 to honor the geographer-explorer Amerigo Vespucci, and he thereby, with the help of Mercator and others, named the continents of the Western Hemisphere before he corrected the misdesignation.[7]

Much of the same information in a relatively similar configuration appears on the 1638 map, "Nova Totius Terrarum . . . ," by the

Plate 5.1. Matthias Quad von Kinckelbach, *Tvpvs Orbis Terrarvm, ad Imitationem Vniversalis Gehardi Mercatoris*. In *Geographisch Handtbuch* (Cologne, 1600). Courtesy of the Cartographic Collections of Mrs. Jenkins Garrett, Special Collections Division, The University of Texas at Arlington Libraries.

Plate 5.2. Kinckelbach, detail.

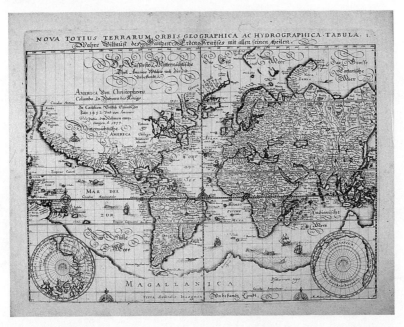

Plate 5.3. Matthäus Merian, *Nova Totius Terrarum Orbis Geographica ac Hydrographica Tabula* (Frankfurt, 1638). Courtesy of the Cartographic Collections of Mrs. Jenkins Garrett, Special Collections Division, The University of Texas at Arlington Libraries.

German engraver-publisher Matthäus Merian (plates 5.3, 5.4).[8] In addition, Cíbola seems to be located on the Colorado River, and, perhaps most interesting, the Rio Grande flows in the wrong direction and into the Sea of Cortés. Although less decorative and minus the Amerindian portraits, the Americas on this map were in turn derived from the current New World map by Willem Blaeu, the "Americae nova tabula" of 1631, but mistakes in the entrada information were perpetuated by Merian from some other unknown source.[9]

Yet another map in this vein is the beautiful but crude and retrograde (especially when compared to the contemporary work of Guillaume Delisle) "Provinciae Borealis Americae . . . " of 1720 by the Jesuit geographer-mathematician Heinrich Scherer (plate 5.5, page 105; plate 5.6).[10] Here California is still an island (having been proven decisively otherwise over two decades previously) and with a

Plate 5.4. Merian, detail.

sea monster offshore. The strait appears on the northwest coast as "Fretvm Anian." The lands of Anian, Totonteac, and Quivira are on the coast. The Cibolan domains, including Acoma, Zuñi, and "Tigvez," are near the coast and strangely located to the northwest of Santa Fe. Scherer covered up the rest of his ignorance about the interior with profuse generic landforms and vegetation.[11]

On Johann Baptist Homann's spectacular hemispheric world map of 1732, the Strait of Anian runs to the north of an insular California and separates it from a vague Arctic landmass while Quivira is to the north of Santa Fe as it is also on his New Spain map of 1763.[12] On a derivative map, George Matthäus Seutter's "Novus Orbis sive America . . . " of 1750, the Homann entrada misinformation is reproduced, and what should be the Columbia River is mislabeled the "Anian R." Perhaps the strait thus was indicated as a possible northwest passage.[13] And Quivira moved north almost into western Canada on the "Carte d'Amerique . . . ," derived from Delisle, by J. A. Dezauche in 1785.[14]

Plate 5.6. Scherer, detail.

The maps of the French royal geographer Didier Robert de Vaugondy, for example, his "Carte des parties nord et ouest de l'Amérique . . . " (1772), place the "Détroit d'Anian" farther north than most others, closer to the location of the actual Bering Strait. Anian and Quivira are located to the south, still on the coast.[15] In another map of 1772, "Carte de la Californie . . . ," Vaugondy shows Quivira to the northeast of Cape Fortuna (plate 5.7, page 105).[16] Inset on this map is another map, done in 1612 by Claes Janszoon Visscher of Amsterdam and first published in 1641, on which Vaugondy's map is based. In their southeast quadrants, both the map and the inset show the Seven Cities of Cíbola around an unnamed lake and along an unnamed river from the lake leading to the Colorado River and into the Sea of Cortés. This composite was created for the atlas of Denis Diderot's *Encyclopédie* (1770–79) and was to show the development of the current state of geographic knowledge about Spanish California.[17]

In 1780, Antonio Zatta, a Venetian map publisher, issued his "America Settentrionale . . . ," based on the maps of Robert de Vaugondy, with Anian inland and Quivira on the coast.[18] He also showed two straits of Anian, one to the north between Asia and North America and the other approximately at the latitude of the Columbia River. The two seem to join deep in the interior to form part of a possible northwest passage. Between the two openings Zatta also recognized Vitus Bering and Alexie Chirikov for having explored this coast in 1741.

One of the last maps to perpetuate the misinformation stemming from the sixteenth century was the "Karte von Amerika . . . " (1795) by the Viennese mapmaker, publisher, and art dealer Franz Johann Joseph von Reilly.[19] In an inset the straits far to the north are still called "Anian" or "Cook's," but not after Bering. Quivira exists to the northwest of "Zuni oder Cibola." Hawikuh and the other villages that made up the so-called seven Cities of Cíbola were finally abandoned during the Pueblo Revolt in 1680. The present pueblo of Zuñi was built on the site of one of the original villages in about 1695. Indicating a form of "Zuni oder Cibola" eventually became quite common and is an example of a cartographic informational transition employed to be geographically "current" while still referencing the popular European-Amerindian myth-history of the region for the viewer. The use of it here is nevertheless somewhat late.

Von Reilly's map (and Zatta's as well) was intended to make money for its publisher and to stimulate interest in the Americas, particularly the eastern seaboard of North America. It is related, therefore, to the somewhat later genres of booster and immigrant maps. That this map is, given its principal purpose and projected audience, more accurate for the East Coast and the eastern Caribbean than the Greater Southwest is then perhaps reasonable. And these eastern areas were by the late eighteenth century still much better explored and revealed than the southwestern interior and eastern Pacific Rim.

Shortly after the reconnaissance attendant to the founding of the capital of Nuevo Mexico, first at San Juan (the pueblo of Ohke) at the confluence of the Chama and the Rio Grande and then at nearby San Gabriel (Yanque) by Juan de Oñate in 1598–99 and at Santa Fe by his successor, Pedro de Peralta, in 1610, the century of the great entradas drew to a close and there ensued a hiatus of concerted Spanish exploration of the southwestern interior, lasting over a century. While these conquistadors had begun to set the parameters and detail the hinterland of a new continent for the Old World, much of what was sought remained elusive and much of what was found seemed to be of little value. Old World notions often found difficult applications to alien New World geography, yielding false hopes, misunderstanding, and disillusionment. Clarification came slowly.

This gap in Spanish exploration may help to explain the continued presence of some of the misinformation transmitted by many post entrada European maps of the Greater Southwest. But another reason may be that the Spanish carefully guarded their knowledge of the interior. Consequently, most Spanish printed maps of this period are not much more than outline layouts, showing coastal detail and little else (see plate 5.8).[20]

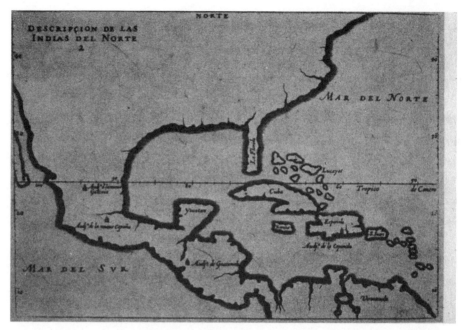

Plate 5.8. Antonio de Herrera y Tordesillas, *Descripción de las Yndias del Norte*. In *Descripción de las Yndias Occidentalis* (Madrid, 1601). Courtesy of the Special Collections Division, The University of Texas at Arlington Libraries.

It was not until the early eighteenth century that the Spanish again seriously began to explore the far reaches of the Greater Southwest. Spain was experiencing stiff competition for empire from France, England, and Holland in Europe, Asia, and the Americas. Accordingly, the Spanish Southwest suffered the accretion of French Louisiana, emanating from the valleys of the Mississippi and Red rivers and from the gulf coast in actuality and on the maps of such prominent cartographers as Vincenzo Maria Coronelli, Delisle, and Herman Moll.[21]

The Spanish eventually were forced by these real and paper-and-print onslaughts to reinforce their claims. Thus Spain gradually revitalized its exploration and settlement inland and produced current maps of its own for publication. Much of the interior nevertheless remained a great mystery on all European printed maps until the nineteenth century.

This enigma is perhaps still best reflected on one of the most important and dominant North American maps of the last half of the seventeenth century, Nicolas Sanson's "Ameriqve Septentrionale . . . " (1650) (plate 5.9, page 106; plate 5.10, page 106).[22] Many of the charming eccentricities of this map by the French royal geographer stem from its combining older geography with newer factual information and because, as one author has pointed out, Sanson was really "an antiquarian by nature and a cartographer by necessity."[23] The Canadian information on this map is most accurate and was based partially on contemporary French missionary reports; the sources for the Spanish Southwest are for the most part earlier maps such as Henry Briggs's "The North Part of America . . . " (1625) and those of Joannes de Laet.[24]

Off the West Coast, California is an island (a Sanson characteristic), and the Rio Grande still flows to the southwest into what would be the Sea of Cortés. "Cibola" and "Zuny" are indicated, and then a second "Cibola" is placed to the north in the vast unknown (by 1656, this Cíbola was eliminated on Sanson's map "Noveau Mexique et la Floride"). "Quivira" is located at the headwaters of a river, presumably the Arkansas, to the southeast of the Nuevo Mexico settlements. "S.Fe" is shown as the capital of "Nueuo Mexico" but located on the west bank of the Rio Grande (Sanson was perhaps confusing the location of Santa Fe with that of San Juan) and to the southeast of "Cibola" and "Zuny." Yet, despite its problems, Sanson's "Ameriqve Septentrionale . . . " was better then many of its contemporaries, for example, Blaeu's "Nova Totius Terrarum" of 1649.[25]

Although the English cartographer John Senex used information from the maps of Delisle and Baron Lahonton (of questionable accuracy) for parts of the "Canada or New France" and "Florida" sections of his map, "North America . . . " (1710), his sources for "New Mexico" are again less discernible.[26] He was known for publishing maps based on captured Spanish charts supplied by English pirates such as William Dampier and Woodes Rogers, but what roles such documents may have played in his portrayal of the Southwest are unclear.[27]

Senex's map has "Zuni or Cibola," and "Quivira" lying to the north of "Taos," marked as a mission where there was none, in the lands of "Incognita." "El Passo" on the Rio Grande on the major route between Mexico City and Santa Fe, traveled by Oñate a century before, also is designated. In the middle of what would become Texas is indicated "this Country is full of Herds of wild Bulls." In fact, many maps of this area from this time, especially those by Moll, carry notations of the presence of "beeves."[28] These could refer to Spanish cattle gone feral—famous Texas longhorns of the nineteenth century—or more probably to the buffalo first sighted by Cabeza de Vaca, who in 1534, not knowing what they were, called them "cattle" or "cows."[29]

On a much later map, "Amerique Septentrionale . . . " (1792) published by Jan Barend Elwe in Amsterdam, "Quivira" is in the proper place, but "Zuni ou Cibola" is in a more peculiar location in the Mogollon Mountains.[30] For a map this late, it also is strange to see the Rio Grande still flowing in the wrong direction. There is nothing really original about this map; it is mostly copied from Reiner and Joshua Ottens's *Atlas Minor . . .* (1723) and also is based on a similar Sanson-Jaillot map from the 1689 edition of the famous *Atlas Nouveau.*[31] Clearly this is another map publisher eschewing current accuracy but nevertheless influencing his public's perception of the Greater Southwest.

This was also probably the case with the German cartographer Christian Gottlieb Reichard's "Charte von Nordamerica . . . " published in Weimar in 1802 (plates 5.11, 5.12).[32] "Quivira" is a vast open space in the West, and it is quite late for only "Cibola" to appear on a map.

The reasons for the prolonged portrayal of entrada data on European maps, often as misinformation, into the nineteenth century are manifold and of consequence. Certainly, the most important reason was simply ignorance of the region. After the passage of the age of the three great Spanish entradas, cartographers lacked the facts to be more accurate. For the next two hundred years the Southwest was given a lower priority by the Spanish for exploration and

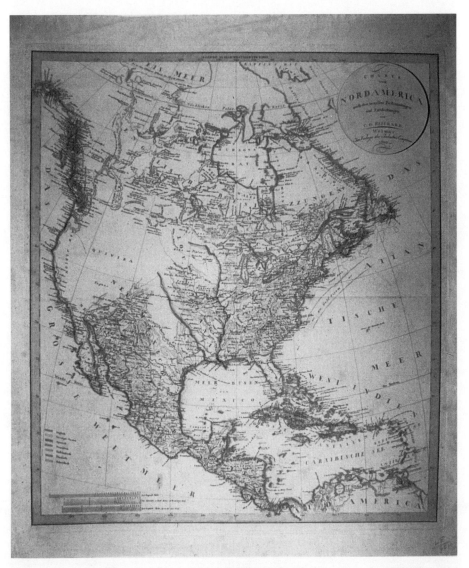

Plate 5.11. Christian Gottlieb Theophil Reichard, *Charte von Nordamerica nach den neusten Bestimmungen und Entdeckungen* (Weimar, 1802). Courtesy of the Cartographic Collections of Mrs. Jenkins Garrett, Special Collections Division, The University of Texas at Arlington Libraries.

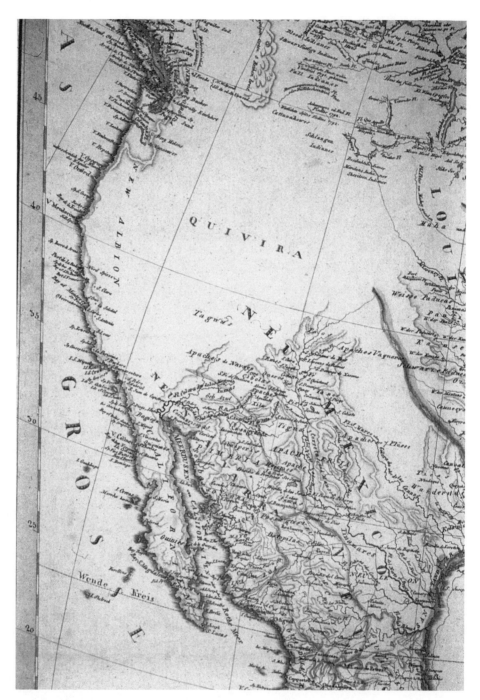

Plate 5.12. Reichard, detail.

settlement in favor of developing the wealth and productivity of Mexico, the Caribbean Basin, and areas of South America.

What geographic knowledge the Spanish had about the northern interior or elsewhere in their empire also was closely guarded and rationed for dissemination. Sometimes it was knowingly issued incorrect or altered for the purposes of disinformation in this first period of European competition for empire.

Thus, although accuracy is historically relative, mapmakers nevertheless found it especially difficult to be precise in their own times about the Greater Southwest. Good information was hard to come by, and the available information was usually colored by a composite of Old World notions held by the cartographers' sources, the cartographers themselves, and their audiences.

The Greater Southwest was of a lower priority for European mapmakers, too. The New World was news.[33] Any information about it was in demand, but exact information about more valuable and exciting regions of the Americas than the disappointing Southwest came into even greater demand by the public. And demand sold maps! In the map trade, therefore, the commercial impulse often won out rather easily over the quest for scientific verity.

This neglect of a truer and more detailed picture of the Greater Southwest by cartographers in part led Europeans to imagine it as a vast, harsh, monotonous, and worthless wasteland lying between the Missouri-Mississippi system to the east, the Pacific Ocean to the west, and the lush heartland of Mexico to the south. This public opinion in turn influenced the priorities and policies of governments that accounted for the comparatively late European exploration and exploitation of the area. It was thereby also left more available to American imperialism in the nineteenth century. In the process, during this period of the ongoing isolation of the region relatively large Amerindian populations (e.g., the Navajo) found refuge and survived there and culturally interacted with its Spanish minority. But perhaps most important, this rather vague Old World view allowed for the perpetuation of some of the European-Amerindian myth-history (e.g., "Aztlan") of the Greater Southwest that has contributed to defining the region today and its significant influence on contemporary American culture.

NOTES

1. George Parker Winship, *The Coronado Expedition, 1540–1542* (Chicago: Rio Grande Press, 1964), 88. Also see A. Grove Day, *Coronado's Quest: The Discovery of the Southwestern States* (Berkeley: University of California Press, 1964); Cleve Hallenbeck, *Alvar Nuñez Cabeza de Vaca: The Journey and Route of the First European to Cross the Continent of North America, 1534–1536* (Port Washington, N.Y.: Kennikat Press, [1940] 1971); Jerald T. Melanich and Susan Milbrath, eds., *First Encounters: Spanish Exploration in the Caribbean and the United States, 1492–1570* (Gainesville: University of Florida Press, 1989); Dennis Reinhartz, " '*Hacia el Norte!*' (To the North!): The Spanish *Entrada* into North America," in *North America Exploration*, edited by John L. Allen (Lincoln: University of Nebraska Press, 1993), 1; and Stuart L. Udall, *To the Inland Empire: Coronado and Our Spanish Legacy* (New York: Doubleday, 1987).

2. Bernard DeVoto, *The Course of Empire* (Cambridge, Mass.: Riverside Press, 1952), 54–55.

3. Ibid., 52–57, 61–63. Also see Reinhartz, " '*Hacia el Norte!*' "

4. The maps cited are all part of the collections of the Cartographic History Library (CHL) at The University of Texas at Arlington, Mrs. Jenkins Garrett (VGC) of Fort Worth, or the author (DJR).

5. Duncan Castlereagh, *The Great Age of Exploration* (London: Reader's Digest Association, 1971), 127–29, 18l; and DeVoto, *The Course of Empire*, 62-63, 284–85.

6. Matthias Quad von Kinckelbach, "Typvs Orbis Terrarvm, Ad Imiationem Vniversalis Gehardi Mercatoris," in *Geographisch Handtbuch* (Cologne, 1600); VGC #00061/51. Because of the retouched picture of Christ, this is probably an example of the second state of this map. See Rodney W. Shirley, *The Mapping of the World: Early Printed World Maps, 1472–1700* (London: Holland Press, 1983), 216–17; and Henry R. Wagner,

Cartography of the Northwest Coast of America to the Year 1800 (Amsterdam: N. Israel, [1937] 1968), 296.

7. See Katherine R. Goodwin and Dennis Reinhartz, *Terra Tabula Nova* (Dallas: Somesuch Press, 1992). Limited edition miniature book.

8. Matthäus Merian, *Nova Totius Terrarum Orbis Geographica ac Hydrographica Tabula* (Frankfurt, 1638); VGC.

9. Willem J. Blaeu, *Americae Nova Tabula* (Amsterdam, 1631); VGC. Also see Shirley, *The Mapping of the World*, 345, 381.

10. Heinrich Scherer, *Provincia Borealis Americae non ita Pridem Detecitae avt Magis ab Evropaeis Excvltae* (1720); VGC #00390/24.

11. Pierluigi Portinaro and Franco Knirsch, *The Cartography of North America, 1500–1800* (New York: Harry N. Abram, 1980), 224.

12. Johann Baptist Homann, *Planiglobii Terrestris cum Utroq Hemisphaerio Calesti Generalis Exhibitio* (Nuremberg, 1732); VGC #00478/49. Also see Johann Baptist Homann, "Regni Mexicani seu Novae Hispaniae Ludovicianae, N. Angliae, Carolinae, et Pensylvaniae," in *Atlas Geographicus Major* (Nuremberg, 1763); VGC #00478/49. Also see Woodbury Lowery, *The Lowery Collection: A Descriptive List of Maps of the Spanish Possessions within the Limits of the United States, 1502–1820* (Washington, D.C.: Government Printing Office, 1912), 332.

13. George Matthäus Seutter, *Novus Orbis sive America Meridionalis et Septentrionalis per Sua. Regna Provincias et Insulas Iuxta Observationes et Descriptiones Recentiss. Divisa et Adornata Cura et Opera* (1750); VGC.

14. J. A. Dezauche, *Carte d'Amerique* (Paris, 1785); CHL #700013/12.

15. Didier Robert de Vaugondy, *Carte des Parties Nord et Ouest de l'Amérique dressee d'Apres les Relations les plus Authentiques, 1764* (Paris, 1772); VGC #00065/8.

16. Didier Robert de Vaugondy, *Carte de la Californie et des Pays Nord-Ouest separes de l'Asie par le detroit de Anian, extraite de deux publices au commencement du 17 Siècle par le S. Robert de Vougondy Geog. ord. du Roi du feu Roi de Pologne Duc de Lorraine et de Bar et de l'Acacemie royale des Sciences et Belles-lettres de Nanci, et Censeur royal* (Paris, 1772); DJR.

17. Carl I. Wheat, *Mapping the Transmississippi West* (San Francisco: Institute of Historical Cartography, 1957), 1:221.

18. Antonio Zatta, "America Settentrionale Divisia ne' fuoi Principali Stati," in *Atlante Novissimo* (Venice, 1775–85), 4; CHL #190032/13. Also see Wheat, *Mapping the Transmississippi West*, 1:148, 236.

19. Franz Johann Joseph von Reilly, *Karte von Amerika* (Vienna, 1795); VGC #00464/61.

20. For example, see Antonio de Herrera y Tordesillas, "Descripción de las Yndias del Norte," in *Descripción de las Indias Occidentalis* (Madrid, 1601). Also see James C. Martin and Robert Sidney Martin, *Maps of Texas and the Southwest, 1513–1900* (Albuquerque: University of New Mexico Press, 1984), 76–77.

21. For example, see Guillaume Delisle, *Carte de la Louisiane et du Cours du Mississipi Dresse sur un grand nombre de Memou es entrau tres fur ceux de M. le Maue Par: Giull aume Delisle del Academie R. des Scien* (Paris, 1718); or Herman Moll, "A New Map of the Parts of North America claimed by France under ye Names of Louisiana, Mississippi, Canada and New France with ye adjoyning territories of England and Spain," in *The New World Described: Or, A New and Correct Sett of Maps* (London, 1726). Also see Dennis Reinhartz, "Herman Moll, Geographer: An Early Eighteenth-Century View of the American Southwest," in *The Mapping of the American Southwest*, edited by Dennis Reinhartz and Charles C. Colley (College Station: Texas A&M University Press, 1987), 18–36, 79–83.

22. Nicolas Sanson, *Ameriqve Septentrionale* (Paris, 1650); VGC #00062/37. Also see Seymour I. Schwartz and Ralph E. Ehrenberg, *The Mapping of America* (New York: Harry N. Abrams, 1980), 112.

23. Lloyd A. Brown, *The Story of Maps* (New York: Dover, 1977), 241. Also see Wheat, *Mapping the Transmississippi West*, 1:39.

24. Schwartz and Ehrenberg, *The Mapping of America*, 111.

25. Wheat, *Mapping the Transmississippi West*, 1:40.

26. John Senex, Charles Price, and John Maxwell, "North America Corrected from the Observations Communicated to the Royal Society at London and the Royal Academy at Paris," in *A New General Atlas* (London, 1721); VGC #00551/64. Also see Wheat, *Mapping the Transmississippi West*, 1:62.

27. Brown, *The Story of Maps*, 9.

28. For example, see Moll, "A New Map of the Parts of North America claimed by France. . . ."

29. Thomas Buckingham Smith, trans., *The Relation of Alvar Núñez Cabeza de Vaca* (Ann Arbor: University Microfilms, 1966), 106–7.

30. Ian B. Elwe, *Amerique Septentrionale Divisee en Ses Principales Parties* (Amsterdam, 1792); VGC #00457/48.

31. Lowery, *Lowery Collection*, 428.

32. Christian Gottlieb Theophil Reichard, *Charte von Nordamerica nach den Neueften Befrimmungen und Entdeckungen* (Weimar, 1802); VGC #00340/61.

33. See *Encountering the New World, 1493–1800*, produced by the John Carter Brown Library, 13 min., 1992, videocassette; and Susan Danforth, ed., *Encountering the New World, 1493–1800* (Providence, R.I.: John Carter Brown Library, 1991).

VI. ENTRADA

The First Century of Mapping the Greater Southwest, An Exhibition

Katherine R. Goodwin

The Columbian encounter in 1492 marked the beginning of a great cartographic adventure. Science and technology combined with exploration and discovery to radically change the European worldview and its expression cartographically. Nowhere is this more apparent than in the maps and charts depicting the region that today encompasses northern Mexico, Texas, and the American Southwest—an area some label the Greater Southwest.

The exhibition examined the evolution of the European perception of the Greater Southwest in maps and charts. The cartographic works that were included in the exhibition date from the fifteenth to nineteenth century but focus primarily on the Spanish encounters in the New World in the sixteenth century. The materials described below include books and graphics, and maps.

THE WORLD BEFORE COLUMBUS

Medieval Europe was hampered in its efforts to undertake maritime voyages of discovery because of rudimentary navigational science. The mariner's compass came into general use only in the fourteenth century, and a seagoing version of the astrolabe, an instrument capable of plotting latitude, was not widely available until the fifteenth century. Indeed, large ships for long ocean voyages were not developed before the fifteenth century.

On the eve of the voyages of Columbus, Europeans held a world-view based on the teachings of the second-century mathematician and astronomer Claudius Ptolemy, who concluded the earth was a sphere approximately 18,000 miles in circumference which held the continents of Europe, Africa, and Asia. Fifteenth-century cartography was dominated by Ptolemy's theories on mapmaking as well as Christian theology. The first maps that emerged from the early years of exploration embraced an allegorical worldview or were of a practical nature for use by mariners.

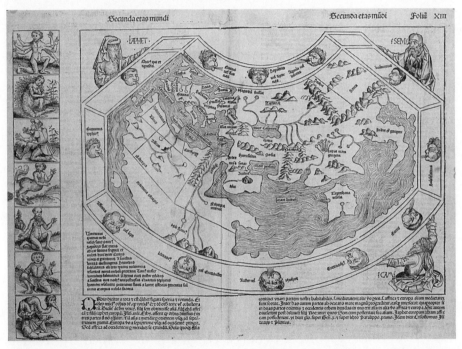

Plate 6.1. [*World, 1493*], by Hartmann Schedel. Nuremberg, 1493. Special Collections Division, The University of Texas at Arlington (hereafter UTA) Libraries.

The world map originally published in the *Nuremberg Chronicle* is based on a simplified Ptolemaic concept that reflects a popularized history of the world. The map was adapted to conform to a "Divine Order of Time." It is a historical reconstruction of the ancient world near the time of creation and a metaphor for the biblical theory of world colonization. The three sons of Noah are seen as the progenitors of the peoples of Europe, Asia, and Africa after the flood. After 1492 the worldview would have to assimilate a fourth race and a fourth continent.

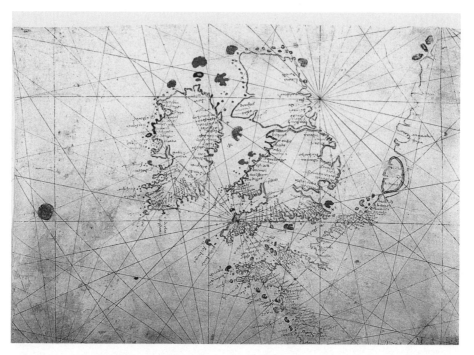

Plate 6.2. "[British Isles Portolan Chart]," by Battista Agnese. Venice, ca. 1540. Special Collections Division, UTA Libraries.

Of more practical use were cartographic innovations from the fourteenth-century portolan charts. Originally developed by Roman traders and navigators of Peripli, they were sets of sailing directions—not maps in the graphic sense—for the use of seamen. The directions gave details of coastlines and islands. The information was gradually transferred to drawings on parchment, thus becoming some of the first scientifically constructed maps.

Portolan charts also reinforced the convention of orienting north at the top of a map. It is believed to be a practical consideration as portolan charts developed about the same time as the discovery of the use of magnets for geographic direction. Simple compasses were made when it was determined that a lodestone attracted iron and that attractive power could be transferred to steel or hardened iron. In turn, the magnetized iron or steel when allowed to float free would then indicate north.

Plate 6.3. *Totivs Partis Habitata Congitae Que Terrae Descriptio*, Vatican Codex. Rome, 1472. Facsimile by Johnson Reprint Corporation, 1983. Cartographic Collections of Mrs. Jenkins Garrett, Fort Worth, Texas.

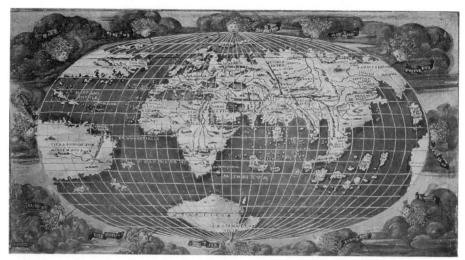

Plate 6.4. [*World, ca. 1508*], by Francisco Rosselli. Florence, ca. 1508. Facsimile by the National Maritime Museum, 1986. Special Collections Division, UTA Libraries.

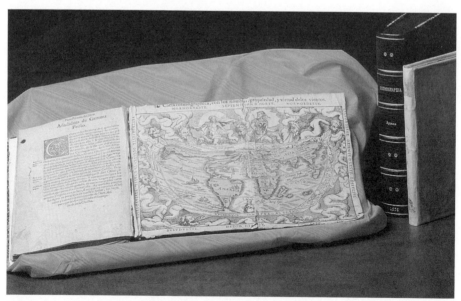

Plate 6.5. *Carta Cosmographica*, by Gemma Frisius. In *Cosmographia de Pedro Apiano, Corregida y Añadida por Gemma Frisio*. Anvers: Juan Bellero al Aguila de Oro, 1575. Special Collections Division, UTA Libraries.

It is reported that Columbus owned a 1490 edition of Ptolemy's *Geographia* and annotated the included maps. These cartographic resources were instrumental in his calculations for his first voyage. The late J. B. Harley asserted Ptolemy's published work "represented in its knowledge, a new systematic device for controlling the world," which was "appropriated by the power brokers of 15th-century Europe." Columbus's place-names relating to Central America are included, although along the coast of Asia. Rosselli was the first cartographer to use an oval map projection (plate 6.4, page 156).

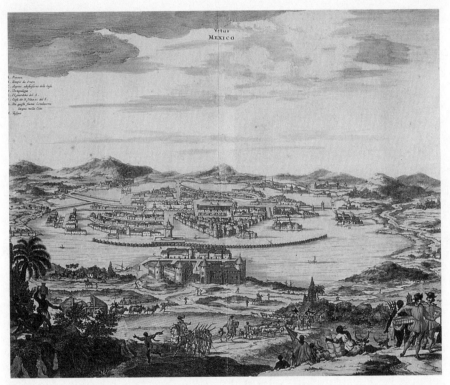

Plate 6.6. *Vetus Mexico*, by John Ogilby. London, 1671. Cartographic Collections of Mrs. Jenkins Garrett, Fort Worth, Texas.

Apian's books were of an encyclopedic nature containing historical, geographic, and quasi-scientific concepts of cosmology. Their popularity helped to spread geographic knowledge of the New World. The world map by Frisius (plate 6.5, page 156) was drawn with North America shown as a slender peninsula.

Plate 6.7. *Libro . . . de tutte l'Isole del Mundo*, by Benedetto Bordone. Venice, 1528. Facsimile by Theatrum Orbis Terrarum, 1966. Special Collections Division, UTA Libraries. *Cosmographia Rome 1478*, by Claudius Ptolemy. Facsimile by Theatrum Orbis Terrarum, 1966. Special Collections Division, UTA Libraries. *Cosmographia Ulm 1482*, by Claudius Ptolemy. Facsimile by Nicole Israel, 1963. Special Collections Division, UTA Libraries. *Geographia Florence 1482*, by Francesco Berlinghieri. Facsimile by Theatrum Orbis Terrarum, 1966. Special Collections Division, UTA Libraries.

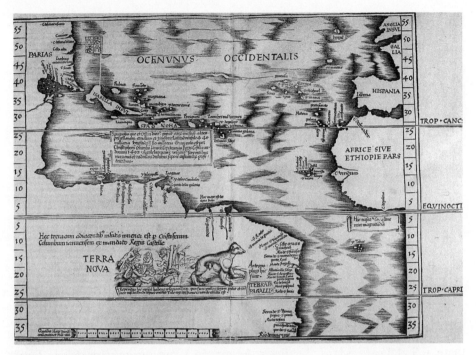

Plate 6.8. *Tabula Terra Nova*, by Martin Waldseemüller. Strassburg, 1523. Special Collections Division, UTA Libraries.

The first printed map devoted exclusively to the New World, this edition is the first to depict New World flora, fauna, and peoples. First published in 1513, the map depicts a fair representation of the gulf coastline several years before Alonso Álvarez de Pineda sailed the perimeter and drew his map in 1519.

Plate 6.9. [*World Map*], by Peter Apian. In *Cosmographicus Liber Petri Apiani Mathematici*, by Peter Apian. Landshut, 1533. Special Collections Division, UTA Libraries.

In describing the advances in the field of astronomy, Apian devised a map with a north polar stereographic projection. The map was a "volvelle," which revealed the revolution of the earth around the polar axis. This popular book was reprinted numerous times over an eighty-year period.

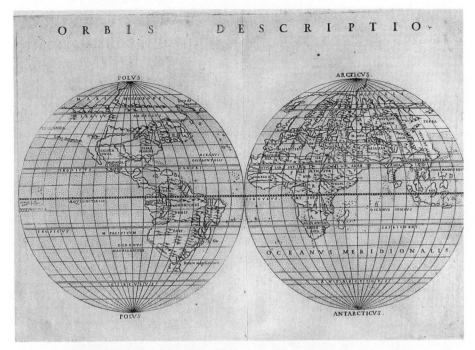

Plate 6.10. *Orbis Descriptio*, by Girolamo Ruscelli. Venice, 1574. Cartographic Collections of Mrs. Jenkins Garrett, Fort Worth, Texas.

Originally produced for the 1561 Ptolemy, Ruscelli, as with a number of his predecessors, joined Asia and America and labeled the northwest coast Litus Incognitum.

CHRISTOFEL COLONUS.

Plate 6.11. *Christofel Colonus*. In *America being the latest and most accurate descriptions* . . . , by John Ogilby. London, 1671. Special Collections Division, UTA Libraries.

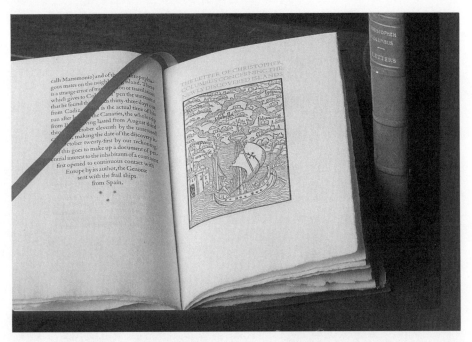

Plate 6.12. Left: *Letter of Christopher Columbus Concerning His First Voyage to the New World Done into English.* Foreword by Donald B. Clark. San Francisco: E. Grabhorn, 1924. Special Collections Division, UTA Libraries. Right: *Select Letters of Christopher Columbus, with Other Original Documents Relating to His Four Voyages to the New World.* Translated and edited by R. H. Major. London: Hakluyt Society, 1847. Special Collections Division, UTA Libraries.

MESO-AMERICAN CARTOGRAPHY

Hernán Cortés and the Europeans who followed him into New Spain found the natives of Mexico with established mapping traditions. The Amerindians of the region were capable of drawings reflecting their ideas about the world and its origin as well as of producing topographic and geographic maps. Over the centuries a fusion of both Amerindian and European forms in mapping emerged in which the European styles dominated.

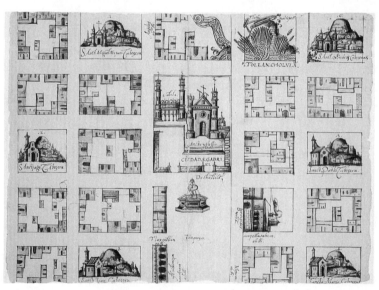

Plate 6.13. Above: "Mapa de Sigüenza," by unknown. Mexico, ca. 1525.
Facsimile from *El territorio mexicano*, by Victor M. Ruiz Naufal et al.
Mexico: Instituto Mexicano del Seguro Social, 1982. Special Collections
Division, UTA Libraries. Below: *Cholula*, by unknown. Mexico, 1581.
Facsimile from *El territorio mexicano*, by Victor M. Ruiz Naufal et al.
Mexico: Instituto Mexicano del Seguro Social, 1982. Special Collections
Division, UTA Libraries.

The *pintura* for *Cholula* (plate 6.13, page 164, below), which accompanied the report of the *corregidor* Gabriel de Rojas of that year, reveals European influences in its general appearance. However, there are still indigenous elements, including the river depiction and the Nahuatl title *Tollan-Cholula* at the top right.

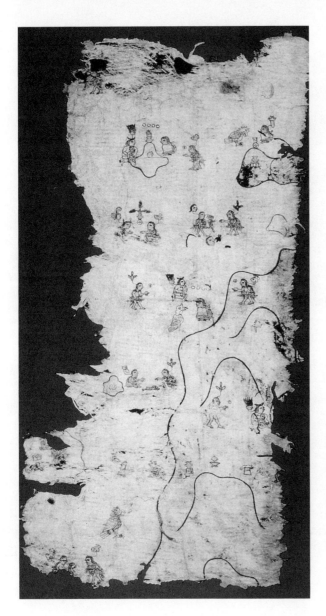

6.14. "Xolotl," by unknown. Mexico, ca. 1525. Facsimile from *El territorio mexicano*, by Victor M. Ruiz Naufal et al. Mexico: Instituto Mexicano del Seguro Social, 1982. Special Collections Division, UTA Libraries.

Representing the most elementary form of Meso-American mapping, the "Xolotl" map (plate 6.14, page 165) interweaves a story with geographic information. It is a simplified version of family visitations and the route they traveled.

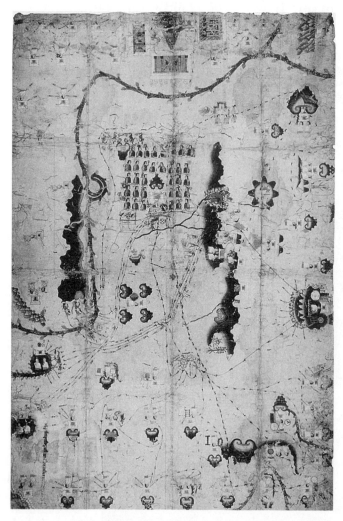

Plate 6.15. "Cuauhtichan No. 1," by unknown. Paris, ca. 1525. Facsimile from *El territorio mexicano*, by Victor M. Ruiz Naufal et al. Mexico: Instituto Mexicano del Seguro Social, 1982. Special Collections Division, UTA Libraries.

"Cuauhtichan No. 1" is an indigenous map of the province of Puebla and the river Atoyac. The river is shown in characteristic Aztec style, and various locations are marked by distinctive glyphs. The locations with arrows indicate areas of conquest. The map depicts the establishment of the Chichimecs' territory (plate 6.15, page 166).

Plate 6.16. *El territorio mexicano*, by Victor M. Ruiz Naufal et al. Mexico: Instituto Mexicano del Seguro Social, 1982. Special Collections Division, UTA Libraries.

The Entradas

Hernan Cortés moved into the Valley of Mexico barely fifteen years after Columbus's last voyage to the New World. Within decades his lieutenants moved northward toward the lands of the Greater Southwest and were soon followed by expeditions led by Alonso Álvarez de Pineda, Hernando de Soto, Pánfilo de Narváez, Fray Marcos de Niza, Francisco Vázquez de Coronado, Juan de Oñate, and others. Along with the wanderings of Alvar Núñez Cabeza de Vaca, these men traveled across a region bounded by present-day Tampa Bay on the east, Baja California on the west, and Kansas on the north. By the end of the sixteenth century Spaniards had explored both coasts and up through the interior of the continent, stamping the land and the maps with an identity that mingled Spanish and American Indian traditions.

Hernán Cortés and Indigenous Mapping

According to David Buisseret, "a considerable number of Spanish descriptions of indigenous maps survived from the period on initial contact, mainly in the writings of Hernán Cortés, Bernal Díaz del Castillo, and Peter Martyr." Díaz del Castillo describes the maps of the coast given to Cortés by the Aztec leader Moctezuma as being produced with great skill.

Plate 6.17. Back row, left, above: *The Fifth Letter of Hernan Cortés to the Emperor Charles V*. New York: B. Franklin, 1970. Special Collections Division, UTA Libraries. Back row, left, below: *The True History of the Conquest of Mexico by Bernal Díaz del Castillo*. London: J. Dean, 1800. Special Collections Division, UTA Libraries. Back row, center (two volumes): *De Orbe Novo: The Eight Decades of Peter Martyr d'Anghera*. New York: G. P. Putnam's Sons, 1912. Special Collections Division, UTA Libraries. Back row, right: *Letters from Mexico*, by Hernan Cortés. Translated by Anthony Pagden. New Haven: Yale University Press, 1986. Special Collections Division, UTA Libraries. Front row, left: *Historia general de las Indias*, by Francisco López de Gómara. Barcelona: Editorial Iberia, 1954. Special Collections Division, UTA Libraries. Front row, right: *Carta Sexta de Hernando Cortés*. New York: S. W. Benedict, 1848. Special Collections Division, UTA Libraries.

Plate 6.18. "*Muteczuma*." In *America, being the latest and most accurate description . . .* , by John Ogilby. London, 1671. Special Collections Division, UTA Libraries.

Plate 6.19. *"Cortés Meeting with Montezuma."* In *The History of the Conquest of Mexico by the Spaniards*, by Antonio de Solis. Translated by Thomas Townsend. London: T. Woodward, J. Hooks, and J. Peele, 1724. Special Collections Division, UTA Libraries.

Plate 6.20. *Universalis Cosmographia*, by Martin Waldseemüller. Straussburg, 1507. Fascimilie reprint, ca. 1980. Cartographic Collections of Mrs. Jenkins Garrett, Fort Worth, Texas.

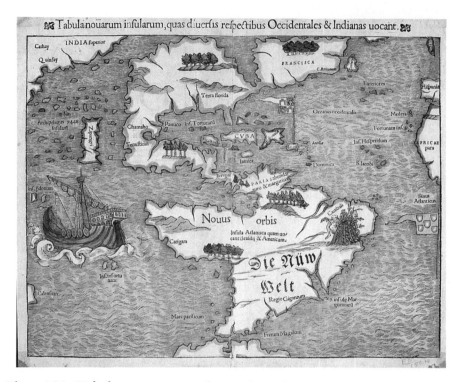

Plate 6.21. *Tabula nouarum insularum,* by Sebastian Petri Münster. Basel, 1550. Cartographic Collections of Mrs. Jenkins Garrett, Fort Worth, Texas.

Tabula nouarum insularum is an early cartographic example indicating that Europe perceived the New World in Old World concepts. In this map Munster depicts the northern continent already divided into Spanish and French territories. The Spanish flag is flying in the Caribbean. Note the vignette of cannibals on the east coast of South America.

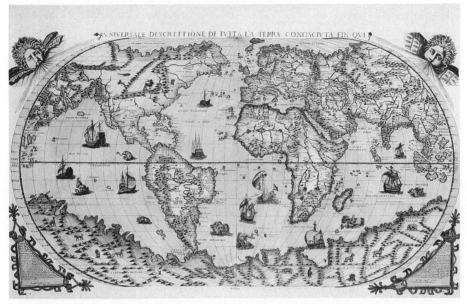

Plate 6.22. *Universale Descrittione di Tutta la Terra Conoscivta Fin Qui,* by P. Forlani and F. Bertelli. Venice, 1565. Facsimile by the National Map Collection, Public Archives of Canada, 1980. Cartographic Collections of Mrs. Jenkins Garrett, Fort Worth, Texas.

Forlani and Bertelli followed the leading Italian mapmaker, Giacomo Gastaldi, in producing this world map. North America and Asia are joined, and Yucatán is an island. Little or no interior data is depicted, but the seas and the far southern landmasses are filled with fanciful creatures.

Plate 6.23. *Nueva Hispania Tabula Nova*, by Girolamo Ruscelli. Venice, 1564. Cartographic Collections of Mrs. Jenkins Garrett, Fort Worth, Texas.

Plate 6.24. *Nueva Hispania Tabula Nova*, by Girolamo Ruscelli. Venice, 1599. Cartographic Collections of Mrs. Jenkins Garrett, Fort Worth, Texas.

Ruscelli, the translator of Ptolemy's work, published the regional map of New Spain—one of the first to focus on a specific area in the New World. The later map depicts the increased information coming from the New World, especially concerning the west coast and the development of the interior (plates 6.23 and 6.24, page 174).

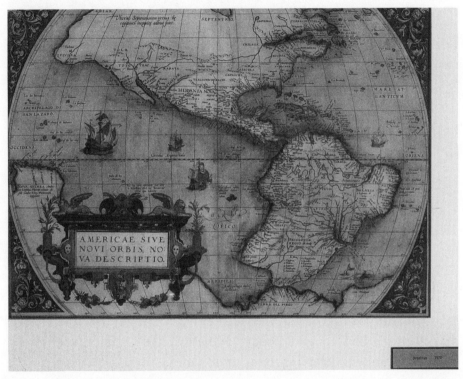

Plate 6.25. *Americae Sive Novi Orbis, Nova Descriptio*, by Abraham Ortelius. Amsterdam, 1570. Special Collections Division, UTA Libraries.

Setting the cartographic standard for the century, Ortelius's popular maps were noted for their reliability, uniformity of size and style, integration of map and text, and the recording of geographic and cartographic sources. His atlases, credited with having great impact on the European image of the New World, were printed forty-one times in seven languages in the last half of the sixteenth century.

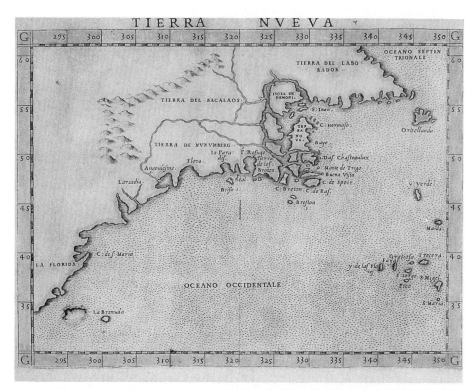

Plate 6.26. *Tierra Nueva*, by Joseph Moletius. Alexandria, 1561. Cartographic Collections of Mrs. Jenkins Garrett, Fort Worth, Texas.

The results of expeditions along the east coast of the continent by Giovanni de Verrazzano (1522–24) are shown by the French names on the New England coast. Moletius, like Ortelius, used every available source to keep his maps up to date.

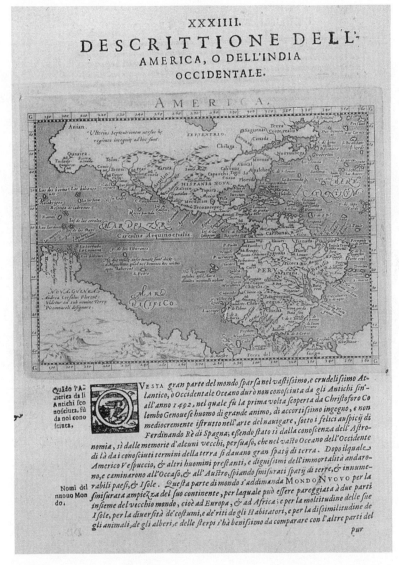

Plate 6.27. *America*, by Giovanni Antonio Magini. Padua, 1620. Special Collections Division, UTA Libraries.

Drawn by the Italian geographer and engraved by Girolamo Porro, this hemispheric view is another of the maps copied from Abraham Ortelius and popularized by Magini. *Entrada* explorations are shown in the place-names from Quivira on the west to Florida on the east.

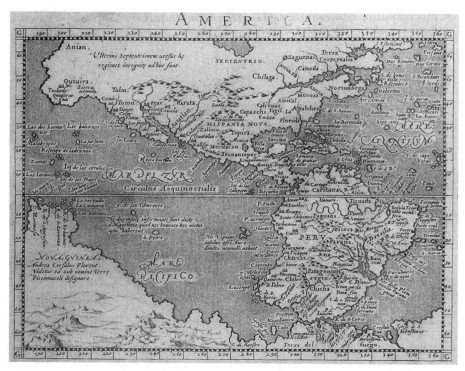

Plate 6.28. *America*, by Giovanni Botero. Rome, 1602. Special Collections Division, UTA Libraries.

Like the Ortelius 1570 map from which it is copied, Botero's *America* records some 2,000 miles of west coast exploration by Francisco de Ulloa, Lucas Vázquez de Ayllón, and others. Place-names include *Sierra Nevada*, *Ingano*, and *Quivira*.

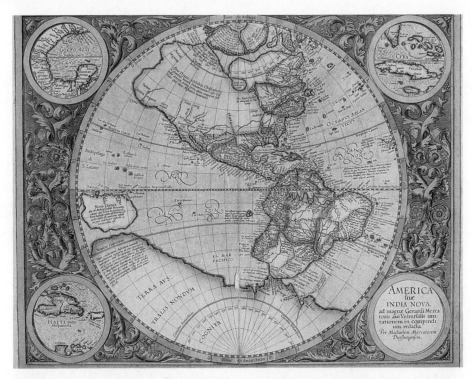

Plate 6.29. *America Sive India Nova*, by Michael Mercator. Dusseldorf, 1595. Cartographic Collections of Mrs. Jenkins Garrett, Fort Worth, Texas.

Like his grandfather, Gerardus, Michael Mercator published numerous editions in at least three languages. This edition gives credence to a northwest passage with the depiction of rivers running across the continent.

Plate 6.30. *Americae Sive Novi Orbis, Nova Descriptio*, by Sebastian Petri
Münster. Basel, 1588. Cartographic Collections of Mrs. Jenkins Garrett,
Fort Worth, Texas.

Reissued and updated by his son, Sebastian Petri, this map was
one of the first to follow the lead of Abraham Ortelius in reporting
New World explorations. The interior of northern New Spain is still
sketchy, but the west coast depicts many more place-names.

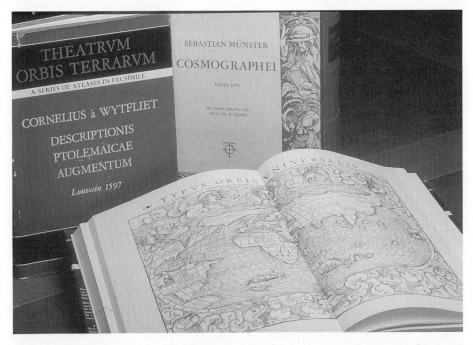

Plate 6.31. Above left: *Descriptionis Ptolemaicae Augmentum, Louvain 1597.* Facsimile by Theatrum Orbis Terrarum, 1964. Special Collections Division, UTA Libraries. Above right: *Geographia, Basle 1540,* by Claudius Ptolemy. Edited by Sebastian Münster. Facsimile by Theatrum Orbis Terrarum, 1966. Special Collections Division, UTA Libraries. Below: *Cosmographei, Basle 1550,* by Sebastian Münster. Facsimile by Theatrum Orbis Terrarum, 1968. Special Collections Division, UTA Libraries.

FLORIDA AND THE EASTERN GULF COAST

Following dreams of conquest and gold, Hernando de Soto and his expedition explored the eastern region of the gulf from Tampa Bay to the Appalachians and into eastern Texas in 1537–43. In the process, he and his men crossed more than three thousand miles, fought many battles with the indigenous peoples, crossed the Mississippi River, penetrated the plains of Oklahoma, and reconnoitered the Arkansas River. Although Soto's travels are depicted in a 1544 manuscript map by Alonso de Santa Cruz, maps by Ortelius in 1584 are some of the first printed items to use place-names from the Soto expedition (plate 6.32, page 182).

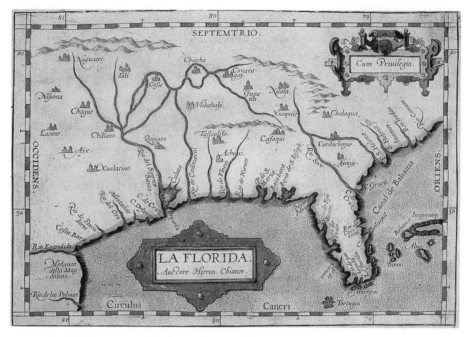

Plate 6.32. *La Florida*, by Gerónimo de Chaves. Amsterdam, 1584. Cartographic Collections of Mrs. Jenkins Garrett, Fort Worth, Texas.

La Florida is attributed to the Spanish pilot major, Gerónimo de Chaves, whom Ortelius tapped for information on the de Soto expedition in Florida.

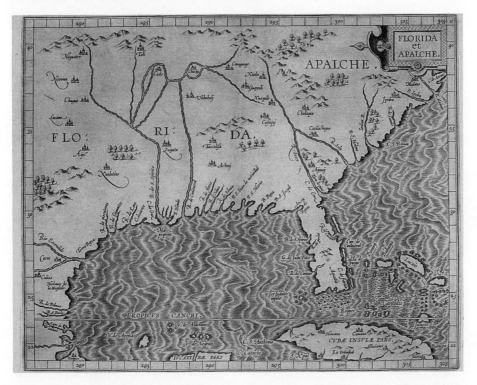

Plate 6.33. *Florida et Apalche*, by Cornelius Wytfliet. Louvain, 1597. Cartographic Collections of Mrs. Jenkins Garrett, Fort Worth, Texas.

This map was included in the first atlas devoted entirely to America and its discovery, natural history, and geography. Wyfliet took years to compile information on the expeditions before publication.

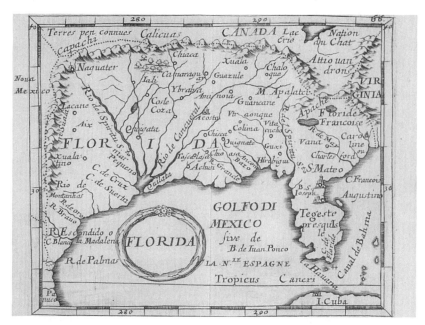

Plate 6.34. *Florida*, by Pierre du Val. Nuremberg, 1682. Special Collections Division, UTA Libraries.

Published in du Val's popular pocket-size geography, *Florida* contains many erroneous conceptions, including Apaches in the Appalachian mountains and numerous rivers in the Mississippi River basin.

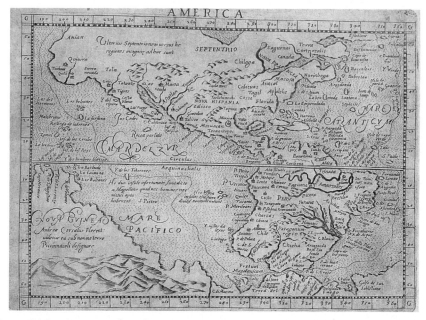

Plate 6.35. *America*, by Giovanni Botero, Cologne, 1598. Special Collections Division, UTA Libraries.

Botero, the German geographer, included this map (plate 6.35, page 184) in his popular geographic and political commentary published in the late sixteenth century. Similar to Abraham Ortelius's 1570 map, Botero's map depicts the west coast expeditions of Francisco de Ulloa and Juan Rodríguez Cabrillo by the inclusion of the place-names *Ingano*, *Quivira*, and *Sierra Nevada* on the coast.

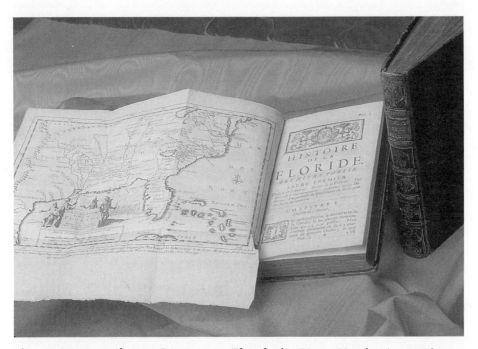

Plate 6.36. *Amerikaans Gewest van Florida*, by Pierre Vander Aa. Leide, ca. 1731. In *Histoire de la Conquête de la Floride*, by Garcilaso de la Vega. Leide, 1731. Special Collections Division, UTA Libraries.

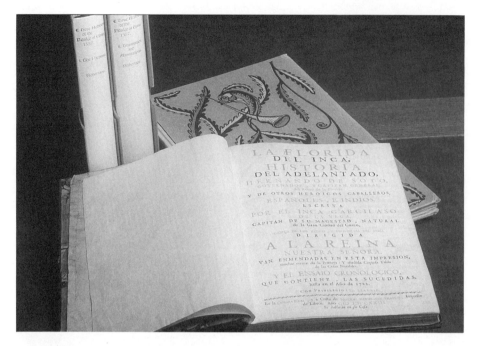

Plate 6.37. Above left (two volumes): *True Relations of the Hardships Suffered by Governor Fernando de Soto . . .* Translated by James Alexander Robertson. Deland: Florida State Historical Society, 1932–33. Special Collections Division, UTA Libraries. Above right: *The Discovery of Florida . . .* San Francisco: Grabhorn Press, 1946. Special Collections Division, UTA Libraries. Below: *La Florida del Inca: Historia del Adelantado, Hernando de Soto, governador y capitan general del reino de la Florida*, by Garcilaso de la Vega. Madrid, 1723. Special Collections Division, UTA Libraries.

CALIFORNIA AND THE WEST COAST

Hernán Cortés sailed up the gulf between Mexico and Lower California in 1539 and named the body of water the Sea of Cortés as he tried to maintain his hold on New World possessions. Initial Spanish exploration of the coast continued with Cortés's deputy, Francisco de Ulloa, and ended with the expeditions of Sebastian Vizcaino in 1602, who sought the elusive Straits of Anian and the mythical city of Quivira. In the ensuing years and decades to follow, the region was the source of much controversy and cartographic manipulation.

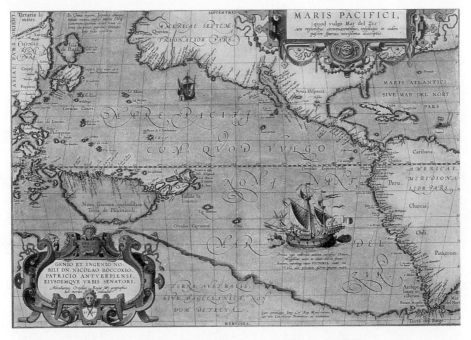

Plate 6.38. *Maris Pacifici*, by Abraham Ortelius. Antwerp, 1590. Cartographic Collections of Mrs. Jenkins Garrett, Fort Worth, Texas.

This map marks a departure for Ortelius. The map still contains place-names associated with Domingo del Costillo, Alarcón's pilot, but with corrections and additions, many from Italian sources. The focus on the Philippine/Japan region also reflects the interest of the period in Far Eastern trade.

Plate 6.39. *America, 1626,* by John Speed. London, 1676. Cartographic
Collections of Mrs. Jenkins Garrett, Fort Worth, Texas.

Engraved by Abraham Goos, the map reveals on the west coast
place-names associated with the account of Juan de Oñate's expedition to the gulf, including Isla de Giganta and the rivers Corall and
Tecon as well as the famous lake of gold.

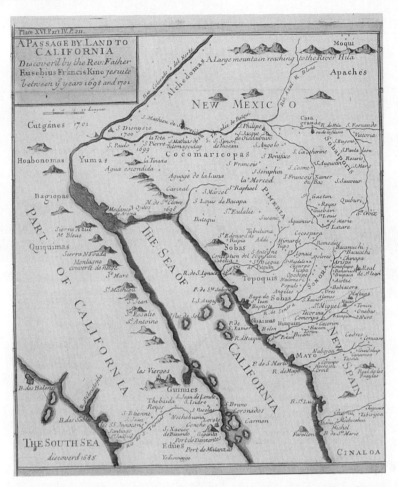

Plate 6.40. *A Passage by Land to California*, by Rev. Father Eusebius Francis Kino. London, ca. 1743. Special Collections Division, UTA Libraries.

Kino explored the Colorado River and northern Sonora area and published maps depicting California as a peninsula. His work, quickly accepted by most cartographers, resulted in the king of Spain declaring in 1746 that California was *not* an island as we commonly depicted at the time. Cartographic depictions of California as an island appear in maps dating generally from 1640 to 1760, but the erroneous assumption was perpetuated even longer by the mapmaker Herman Moll, who asserted he had personally spoken with ship captains who had sailed around the "island."

Plate 6.41. *Americae Descriptio*, by Philippi Chetwind. London, 1666. Special Collections Division, UTA Libraries.

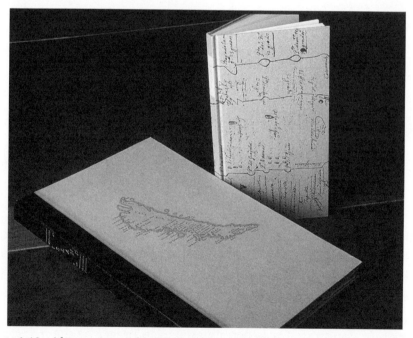

Plate 6.42. Above: *Spanish Approaches to the Island of California*. Translated by W. Michael Mathes. San Francisco: Book Club of California, 1975. Special Collections Division, UTA Libraries. Below: *California as an Island*, by John Leighly. San Francisco: Book Club of California. Special Collections Division, UTA Libraries.

THE LEGACIES

European mapping traditions and perceptions of the Greater Southwest prevailed, and early knowledge of the region gradually reshaped and broadened the worldview. Maps and charts from the seventeenth, eighteenth, and nineteenth centuries continued to reveal these New World perceptions and supported the linkages between the experiences of the early Spanish explorers in the Greater Southwest and the resulting cartographic evidence. The evolving maps are more than cartographic representations of a geographic location in time, or the graphic portrayal of old myths and stories; they are also depictions of the encounter between the Old World and the New World.

Plate 6.43. *Descripción de las Yndias del Norte*, by Antonio de Herrera y Tordesillas. Madrid, 1601. In *Descripción de las Yndias Occidentalis, Historia general de los hechos de los Castellanos en las Islas i Tierra Firme del Mar Oceano*, by Antonio de Herrera y Tordesillas. Madrid, 1601. Special Collections Division, UTA Libraries.

At the turn of the seventeenth century, the Spaniards were still carefully guarding their knowledge of the interior of New Spain, treating such intelligence as state secrets. The Herrera map (plate 6.43, page 191), showing only outlines and a few coastal details, is typical of most Spanish printed works on the period.

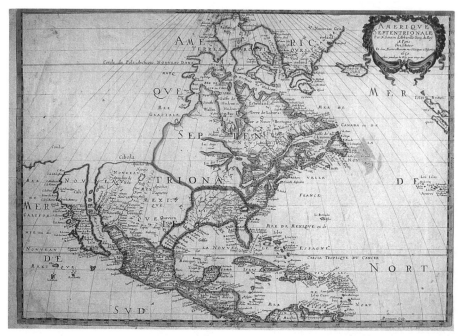

Plate 6.44. *Amerique Septentrionale*, by Nicolas Sanson d'Abbeville. Paris, 1650. Cartographic Collections of Mrs. Jenkins Garrett, Fort Worth, Texas.

One of the most important maps of North America in the last half of the seventeenth century, Sanson's work combines the older geography with newer factual information. The information shown on the northern portion is most accurate as it was based on contemporary French missionary reports. However, in the Spanish Southwest, Sanson had to rely on earlier maps, such as those by Henry Briggs and Johannes de Laet.

Plate 6.45. *North America*, by John Senex, Charles Price, and John Maxwell. In *A New General Atlas*. London, 1710. Cartographic Collections of Mrs. Jenkins Garrett, Fort Worth, Texas.

The English cartographer John Senex was noted for publishing maps based on captured Spanish charts supplied by English pirates. In this 1720 effort, he placed "El Passo" on the Rio Grande along the major route between Mexico City and Santa Fe. In addition, he notes in an area that will become Texas, "this country is full of Herds of Wild Bulls," an observation first reported by Cabeza de Vaca.

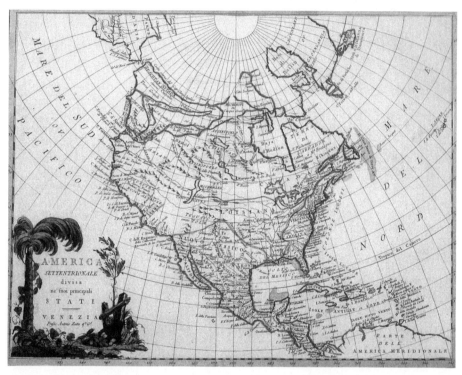

Plate 6.46. *America Settentrionale Divisa né Suoi Principali Stati,* by Antonio Zatta. In *Atlante Novissimo.* Venice, 1775–85. Special Collections Division, UTA Libraries.

By 1780, Antonio Zatta, a Venetian map publisher, depicted *two* Straits of Anian, one in the far north between Asia and North America and the other approximately at the latitude of the Columbia River. According to Dennis Reinhartz, the two appear to join in the interior to form part of a possible northwestern passage.

Plate 6.47. *Typvs Orbis Terrarvm*, by Matthias Quad von Kinckelbach. In *Geographisch Handtbuch*. Cologne, 1600. Cartographic Collections of Mrs. Jenkins Garrett, Fort Worth, Texas.

At the turn of the century, this widely distributed map depicted the Strait of Anian, the lands of Anian Regnum, and Vázquez de Coronado's Quivira, Tiguex, and Axa Tontene. (See also plate 6.48, page 196.)

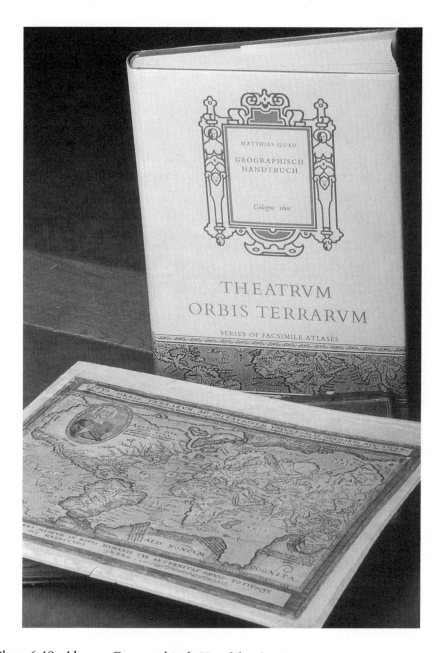

Plate 6.48. Above: *Geographisch Handtbuck, Cologne 1600*, by Matthias Quad von Kinckelbach. Facsimile by Theatrum Orbis Terrarum, 1969. Special Collections Division, UTA Libraries. Below: *Typvs Orbis Terrarvm*, by Matthias Quad von Kinckelbach (Plate 6.47).

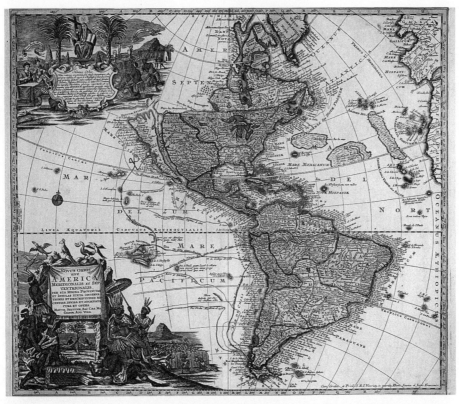

Plate 6.49. *Novus Orbis Sive America,* by George Matthäus Seutter. Augsburg, 1750. Cartographic Collections of Mrs. Jenkins Garrett, Fort Worth, Texas.

Seutter derived entrada misinformation from Johann Baptist Homann's world map of 1732. What should be the Columbia River is labeled "Anian R." and leads the observer to the possibility of a northwestern passage.

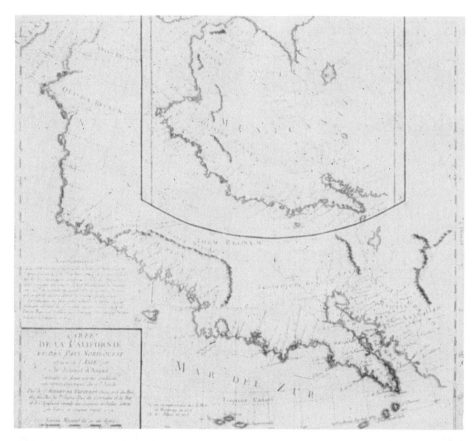

Plate 6.50. *Carte de la Californie et des Pays Nord-ouest*, by Didier Robert de Vaugondy. Paris, 1772. Collection of Judy and Dennis Reinhartz, Arlington, Texas.

Although published the same year as *Cartes des parties*, Vaugondy places Quivira northeast of Cape Fortuna above the fifty-fifth parallel indicating difficulty with obtaining Spanish information on the interior of North America.

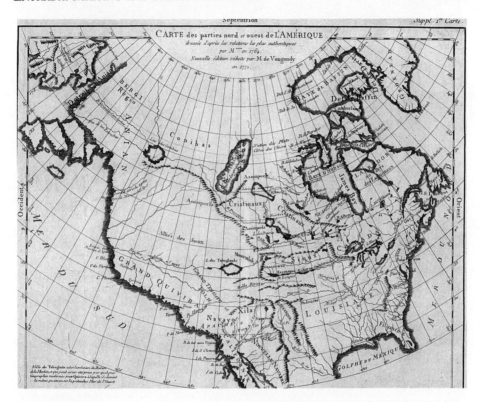

Plate 6.51. *Carte des Parties nord et Ouest de l'Amerique,* by Didier Robert de Vaugondy. Paris, 1772. Cartographic Collections of Mrs. Jenkins Garrett, Fort Worth, Texas.

Geographic myths are prevalent on this map by the French royal geographer, Vaugondy. He has placed Anian farther north than most other cartographers and located Quivira on the southern coast between the fortieth and forty-fifth parallels.

Plate 6.52. *Americae Nova Tabula*, by Willem Blaeu. Amsterdam, 1631. Cartographic Collections of Mrs. Jenkins Garrett, Fort Worth, Texas.

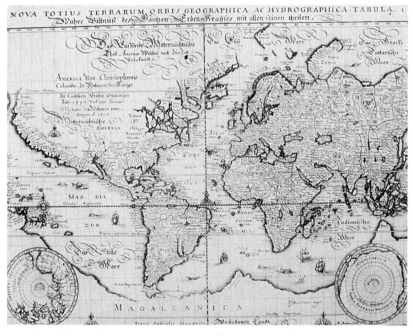

Plate 6.53. *Nova Totius Terrarum Orbis Geographica ac Hydrographica Tabula*, by Matthäus Merian. Frankfurt, 1638. Cartographic Collections of Mrs. Jenkins Garrett, Fort Worth, Texas.

The German engraver Merian perpetuated erroneous entrada information from maps by Willem Blaeu and others. Cíbola is located on the Colorado River and the Rio Grande flows into the Sea of Cortés (plate 6.53, page 200).

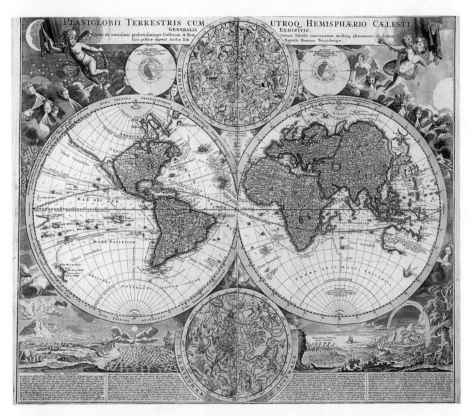

Plate 6.54. *Planiglobii Terrestris cum Utroq Hemisphaerio Calesti Generalis Exhibitio*, by Johann Baptist Homann. Nuremberg, 1732. Cartographic Collections of Mrs. Jenkins Garrett, Fort Worth, Texas.

The twin hemispheres surrounded by smaller projections of the world had become the standard presentation by the early eighteenth century. However, much of the imagery of the Greater Southwest had not changed.

Plate 6.55. *Spanish Colonial Lady, Early 17th Century*, by José Cisneros, 1990. Pen-and-ink drawing on paper. Special Collections Division, UTA Libraries.

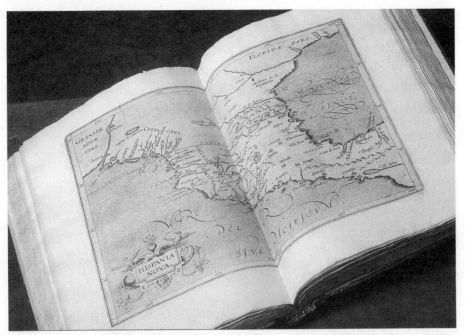

Plate 6.56. *Hispania Nova.* In *Histoire vniverselle des Indes Occidentales et Orientales, et de la conversion indiens,* by Cornelius Wytfliet. Douay: Francisco Fabri, 1611. Special Collections Division, UTA Libraries.

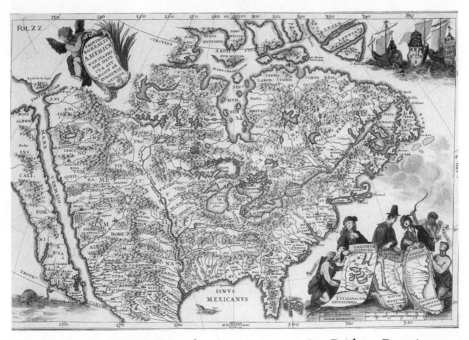

Plate 6.57. *Provinciae Borealis Americae non ita Pridem Detecitae avt Magis ab Eyropaeis Excvitae,* by Heinrich Scherer, 1720. Cartographic Collections of Mrs. Jenkins Garrett, Fort Worth, Texas.

The Jesuit geographer Scherer (see plate 6.57, page 203) continued to portray California as an island more than two decades after it had been proven a peninsula. In addition, Acoma, Zuñi, and Tiguex are mislocated northwest of Santa Fe and near the coast.

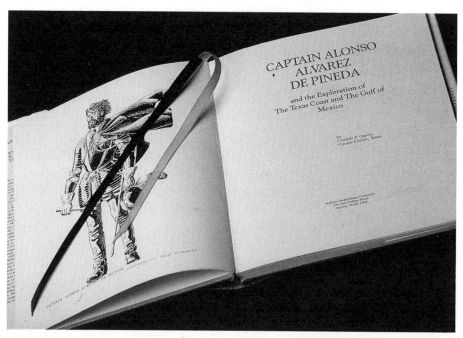

Plate 6.58. *Captain Alonso Álvarez de Pineda and the Exploration of the Texas Coast and the Gulf of Mexico.* Austin: San Felipe Press, 1982. Special Collections Division, UTA Libraries.

Plate 6.59. *Don Hernán Cortés, ca. 1526,* by José Cisneros, 1991. Pen and ink drawing on paper depicting the first conquistador. Special Collections Division, UTA Libraries.

Plate 6.60. *Don Francisco Vásques de Coronado, ca. 1540,* by José Cisneros, 1991. Pen and ink drawing on paper depicting the last conquistador. Special Collections Division, UTA Libraries.

NOTES

The bilingual exhibition, drawing on the collections of the Cartographic History Library, The University of Texas at Arlington Libraries, and the private map collection of Mrs. Jenkins Garrett of Fort Worth, Texas, showcased many important graphic images of the New World printed in Europe from the sixteenth through the nineteenth century and explored the connection between the actual experiences of early Spanish explorers and the maps that reflected the perceptions of the region.

The exhibition was curated and installed by Katherine R. Goodwin, Cartographic Archivist and Exhibits Curator for the Special Collections Division, The University of Texas at Arlington Libraries, in conjunction with the symposium held at the university on February 20, 1992. The division wishes to thank Dr. José Sanchez of the Department of Languages for his advice and counsel regarding Spanish and Mexican-American linguistic and cultural traditions. The inclusion of the text and representative graphics of the exhibition in this publication is made possible by a generous grant from the Graduate School of The University of Texas at Arlington.

CARTOBIBLIOGRAPHY

Katherine R. Goodwin

This cartobibliography has been compiled from the papers presented at the symposium held on Febraury 20, 1992, at The University of Texas at Arlington. Manuscript and printed materials have been combined. Entries are presented with titles of manuscript maps enclosed in quotation marks followed by the name and location of the holding repository. Titles of printed materials are italicized and are followed by place of publication, publisher, and year of publication as known. Both manuscript materials and printed maps without titles have been given a descriptive title that has been placed in brackets.

Aa, Pierre Vander. *Amerikaans Gewest van Florida*. Leide, ca. 1731.

Agnese, Battista. "[British Isles Portolan Chart]." Venice, ca. 1540.

———. "[Southern Part of North America]." In "[Portolan Atlas]," 1557. The Newberry Library, Chicago.

———. "[World Map, 1542]." John Carter Brown Library, Providence, Rhode Island.

Álvarez de Pineda, Alonso. "[Map of the Gulf Coast, 1519, or Traza de las costas de Tierra Firme y de las Tierras Nuevas]." Archivo General de Indias, Seville.

Anonymous. "[Buckinghamshire, England, ca. 1550]." The Huntington Library, San Marino, California.

Anonymous. "Map of Yutzacono and Santa Maria Azompa (Oaxaca), 1698." Archivo General de la Nación, Mexico City.

Anonymous. "[North America, ca. 1536]." In "[World Atlas, ca, 1540]." Koninkliske Bibliotheek, The Hague.

Anonymous. [*World Map, 1534*]. In *Libro primo de la historia de l'Indie Occidentali*. Venice, 1534.

Antonelli, Juan-Bautista. "Map of the Road from Medellín to Mexico City, 1590." Archivo General de Indias, Seville.

Apian, Peter. [*World Map*]. In *Cosmographicus Liber Petri Apiani Mathematici Studiose Collectus*. Landshut, 1533.

Bacon, Roger. "[Spherical Earth]." In "Opus Majus," ca. 1275. British Library, London.

Behaim, Martin. [*Globe, ca. 1492*]. Germanisches Nationalmuseum, Nuremberg.

Bellere, Jean. *Brevis Exactaqe Totius Novi Orbis Eivsor Insularum Descriptio Recens*. In *Historia de México*, by Francisco López de Gómara. Antwerp, 1554.

Berlinghieri, Francesco. *Geografia Florence 1482*. Florence, 1482.

Blaeu, Willem J. *Americae Nova Tabula*. Amsterdam, 1631.

———. *Nova Totius Terrarum*. Amsterdam, 1649.

Bordone, Benedetto. [*World Map*]. In *Libro di Benedetto Bordone nel qual si ragiona de tutte l'Isole del Mundo*. Venice: Nicoló Zoppino, 1528.

Botero, Giovanni. *America*. Cologne, 1598.

———. *America*. Rome, 1602.

Briggs, Henry. *The North Part of America*. In *Hakluytus Posthumus*. London, 1625.

Cabot, Sebastian. [*World Map, 1544*]. Nuremburg, 1544.

Cantino, Alberto. "[World Map, ca. 1502]." Biblioteca Estense, Moderno, Italy.

"Carte Pisane, ca. 1275." Bibliothèque Nationale, Paris.

Castillo, Domingo del. [*Map of California and the Mexican Coast, 1541*]. In *Historia de Nueva España, escrita por su esclarecida conquestador Hernán Cortés*, by Francisco Antonio Lorenzana. Mexico City: Imprenta del Supremo Gobierno, 1770.

"Catalan Atlas, ca. 1375." Bibliothèque Nationale, Paris.

Chaves, Gerónimo de. *La Florida*. In *Theatrum Orbis Terrarum*, by Abraham Ortelius. Amsterdam: Ortelius, 1584.

Cháves, Gabriel de. "Map of Zenpoala, San Miguel, and Suchiguacan (Hidalgo), Mexico, 1589." Archivo General de la Nación, Mexico City.

Chetwind, Philippi. *Americae Descriptio*. London, 1666.

Cholula. Mexico, 1581.

[Cortés, Hernán]. [*Gulf of Mexico, 1524*]. In *Praeclara Fernandi Cortesii de nova Maris Oceani Hyspania narratio*. Nuremberg: Conventum Imperialum, 1524.

[———]. "[Map of California and the Mexican Coast, ca. 1535–39]." Archivo General de Indias, Seville.

Cosa, Juan de la. "[World Map, ca. 1500]." Museo Naval, Madrid.

Covarrubias, Gaspar. "Map of the Lands of Juan de Azanda (Temascaltepec), 1579." Archivo General de la Nación, Mexico City.

"Cuauhtinchan No. 1," ca. 1525. Bibliothèque Nationale, Paris.

Delisle, Guillaume. *Carte de la Louisiane et du Cours du Mississipi Dresse sur un grand nombre de Memou es entrau tres fur ceux*. Paris, 1718.

Dezauche, J. A. *Carte d'Amerique*. Paris: Dezauche, 1785.

du Val, Pierre. *Florida*. Nuremberg, 1682.

"[Egerton MS. 2803, ca. 1510]." British Museum, London.

Elwe, Ian B. *Amerique Septentrionale Divisee en Ses Principales Parties*. Amsterdam: Elwe, 1742.

Finé, Oronce. *Nova, Et Integra Universi Orbis Descriptio, 1531*. Accompanies *Novus Orbis Regionum*, by Johann Huttich and Simon Grynaeus. Basel, 1531.

Forlani, P., and F. Bertelli. *Universalis Descrittione di Tutta la Terra Conoscivta Fin Qui*. Venice, 1565.

Frisius, Gemma. *Carta Cosmographica*. In *Cosmographia de Pedro Apiano, Corregida y Añadida por Gemma Frisio*. Anvers: Juan Bellero al Aguila de Oro, 1575.

García de Toreno, Nuño. [*Map of America and the Atlantic Ocean, 1534*]. John Carter Brown Library, Brown University, Providence, Rhode Island.

————. "[Salviati Planisphere, ca. 1525]." Biblioteca Medicea Laurenziana, Florence.

Gastaldi, Giacomo. *Cosmographia Universalis Et Exactissima Iuxta Postremam Neotericorum Traditionem.* Venice, ca. 1561.

Guerrero y Torres, Francisco Antonio. "Map of Los Reyes, 1783." Archivo General de la Nación, Mexico City.

Gutiérrez, Diego. "Americae sive quarte orbis partis nova et exactissima descriptio," 1562. British Library, London.

Gutiérrez, Sancho. "[Map of the World, ca. 1544–1551]." Österreichische Nationalbibliothek, Vienna.

"Harleian Map, ca. 1536." British Library, London.

Herrera y Tordesillas, Antonio de. *Descripción de las Yndias del Norte.* In *Descripción de las Indias Occidentalis.* Madrid, 1601.

[Higden, Ranulf]. "[Mappaemundi], n.d." British Library, London.

Homann, Johann Baptist. *Planiglobii Terrestris cum Utroq Hemisphaerio Calesti Generalis Exhibitio.* Nuremberg: Homanno, [1732].

————. *Regni Mexicani seu Novae Hispaniae Ludovicianae, N. Angliae, Carolinae, et Pensylvaniae.* In Atlas Geograpicus Major. Nuremberg, 1763.

Homem, Andrés. "Universa ac navigabilis totius terrarum orbis descriptio, 1559." Bibliothèque Nationale, Paris.

Kino, Eusebius Francis. *A Passage by Land to California.* London, ca. 1743.

López de Velasco, Juan. [*Map of North America, ca. 1574*]. In *Geographia y descripción universal de las Indias*, bu Juan López de Velasco. Madrid: Ediciones Atlas, 1971.

Magini, Giovanni Antioio. *America.* Padua, 1620.

"Mapa de Sigüenza," ca. 1525. Biblioteca National de Antropología e Historia, Mexico City.

"Map of Tepetlaoztoc," 1583. In Codex Kingsborough. British Library, London.

"Map of Temascaltepec," ca. 1550. The Newberry Library, Chicago.

"Map of Yutzacomo and Santa Maria Azompa (Oaxaca), 1698." Archivo General de la Nación, Mexico City.

Martellus, Henricus. "[World Map, ca. 1490]." Beinecke Library, Yale University, New Haven.

Martínez, Enrico. "[Map of New Mexico, ca. 1602]." Archivo General de las Indias, Seville.

"Memorial de los Indios de Tepetloaztoc." Codex Kingsborough. British Library, London.

Mercator, Gerhardus. *Nova et Aucta Orbis Terrae Descriptio ad Usum Navigantium Emendate Accommodata.* Duisberg, 1569.

———. *[World Map, 1531].* Louvain, 1538.

Mercator, Michael. *America Sive India Nova.* Dusseldorf, 1595.

Merian, Matthäus. *Nova Totius Terrarum Orbis Geographica ac Hydrographica Tabula.* [Frankfurt: Merian, 1638].

Moletius, Joseph. *Tierra Nueva.* Alexandria, 1561.

Moll, Herman. *A New Map of the Parts of North America claimed by France under ye Names of Louisiana, Mississippi, Canada and New France with ye adjoyning territories of England and Spain.* In *The World Described: Or, A New and Correct Sett of Maps.* London: Moll, 1726.

———. *North America.* London: Moll, 1720.

Morales, Andrés de. *[Map of America].* In *Opera. Legatio babilonica. Occeanea decas. Poemata,* by Peter Martyr. Hispali: Jocabum Corumberger Aleman, 1511.

Morán, Alonso. "Map of Coquila, Oaxaca, Mexico, 1599." Archivo General de la Nación, Mexico City.

Münster, Sebastian Petri. *Americae Sive Novi Orbis, Nova Descriptio.* Basel, 1588.

———. *Tabula nouarum insularum.* Basel: Sebastian Münster, 1550.

Ogilby, John. *Vetus Mexico.* London, 1671.

———. *Christofel Colones.* London, 1671.

Olives, Bartolomé. "Terra Florida." In "[Atlas] 1562," by Bartolomé Olives. Biblioteca Vaticana, Rome.

Ortelius, Abraham. *Americae Sive Novi Orbis, Nova Descriptio.* Amsterdam: Ortelius, 1570.

———. *La Florida.* Amsterdam, 1595.

———. *Maris Pacifici.* Antwerp, 1590.

————. *Theatrum Orbis Terrarum.* Amsterdam: Ortelius, 1570.

Ottens, Reiner, and Joshua Ottens. *Atlas Minor.* Amsterdam, 1723.

"Pintura Atengo." Relación geográficas de Atengo, 1579. Nettie Lee Benson Latin American Library, The University of Texas at Austin.

"Pintura Cholula." Relación geográficas de Cholula, 1581. Nettie Lee Benson Latin American Library, The University of Texas at Austin.

"Pintura Culhuacan." Relación geográficas de Mexicaltino, 1580. Nettie Lee Benson Latin American Library, The University of Texas at Austin.

"Pintura Meztitlan." Relación geográficas de Mextitlan, 1579. Nettie Lee Benson Latin American Library, The University of Texas at Austin.

"Pintura Quautlatlaca." Relación geográficas de Quautlatlaca, 1579. Nettie Lee Benson Latin American Library, The University of Texas at Austin.

"Pintura Teozacoalco." Relación geográficas de Teozacoalco, 1580. Nettie Lee Benson Latin American Library, The University of Texas at Austin.

"Pintura Texúpa." Relación geográficas de Texúpa, 1579. Real Academia de la Historia, Madrid.

"Plano en papel de Maguey." Biblioteca Nacional de Antropología e Historia, Mexico City.

Ptolemy, Claudius. *Cosmographia Rome 1478.* Rome: Arnoldus Buckinek, 1478.

————. *Cosmographia Ulm 1482.* Rome, 1482.

————. [*World Map*]. In Registrum hujus operis libri cronicarum . . . Nuremberg: Hartmann Schedel, 1493.

Quad von Kinckelbach, Matthias. *Typvs Orbis Terrarvm, ad Imiationem Vniversalis Gehardi Mercatoris.* In *Geographisch Handtbuch.* Cologne, 1600.

Reichard, Christian Gottlieb Theophil. *Charte von Nordamerica nach den neusten Bestimmungen und Entdeckungen.* Weimar: Industrie Comploins, 1802.

Ribero, Diego. "[Castiglioni Planisphere, ca. 1525]." Archivo Marchesi, Castiglioni, Mantua.

———. "[World Map, 1527–1529]." Thuringische Landesbibliothek, Weimar.

———. "[World Map, 1529]." Borgiano 3. Biblioteca Vaticana, Rome.

Rojas, Cristóbal de. "Plan of Havana, Cuba, 1603." Archivo General de Indias, Seville.

Rosselli, Francesco. [*World, ca. 1508*]. Florence, ca. 1508.

Ruscelli, Girolamo. *Nueva Hispania Tabula Nova*. Venice, 1564.

———. *Nueva Hispania Tabula Nova*. Venice, 1599.

———. *Orbis Descriptio*. Venice, 1574.

Saavedra Cerón, Alvaro de. "[Map of Santiago, Mexico, ca. 1527]." Relacion del viage q. hizo un bergantin en lo de la mar del sur antes que enbieron los novios. Archivo General de Indias, Seville.

San Agustín, Pedro de. "Pintura Culhuacan." Relación geográficas de Mexicaltingo, 1580. Nettie Lee Benson Latin American Library, The University of Texas at Austin.

Sanson d'Abbeville, Nicolas. *Amerique Septentrionale*. Paris: Sanson, 1650.

———. *Noveau Mexique et la Floride*. Paris: Sanson, 1656.

Santa Cruz, Alonso de. "[De Soto's Map, ca. 1544]." Archivo General de Indias, Seville.

———. "[Gulf of Mexico, ca. 1567]." Archivo Histórico Nacional, Madrid.

———. "Map of Mexico City." University Library, Uppsala, Sweden.

———. "Novus verior et integra totius orbis descriptio nunc primum in lucem edita per Alfonsum de Sancta Cruz Caesaris Charoli, 1542." The Hague, Koninklijke Bibliotheek, Netherlands.

———. "Tenuxtitlan Mexico," 1560. Archivo General de la Nación, Mexico City.

———. "[World Map, 1542]." In "Islario general de todas las islas del mundo." Biblioteca del Palacio Real, Madrid.

Sarmiento de Vera, Bernave. "Map of Ocotlan and Simitlan (Oaxaca), Mexico, 1534." Archivo General de la Nación, Mexico City.

Schedel, Hartman. [*World, 1493*]. Nuremberg, 1493.

Scherer, Heinrich. *Provinciae Borealis Americae non ita Pridem Detecitae avt Magis ab Evropaeis Excvitae*. Scherer, 1720.

Senex, John, Charles Price, and John Maxwell. *North America Corrected from the Observations Communicated to the Royal Society at London and the Royal Academy at Paris*. In *A New General Atlas*. London, 1710.

Seutter, George Matthäus. *Novus Orbis Sive America Meridionalis et Septentrionalis per Sua. Regna Provincias et Insulas Iuxta Observationes et Decriptiones Recentiss. Divisa et Adornata Cura et Opera*. Augsburg, 1750.

Speed, John. *America, 1626*. London, 1676.

———. *Theater of the Empire of Great Britain*. London, 1611.

Tatton, Gabriel. *Nova et rece Terraum [sic] et regnorum Californiae, nouae Hispaniae, Mexicanae, et Peruviae, una cum exacgta absolutaq orarum Sinus Mexicani, ad Insulam Cubam usq Oraeq maritimae ad Mare austraicum delineatio*. London, 1610.

Totivs Partis Habitata Congitae Que Terrae Descriptio. Vatican Codex. Rome, 1472.

Vaugondy, Didier Robert de. *Carte de la Californie et des Pays Nord-ouest separes de l'Asie par le détroit de Anian, extraite de deux publices au commencement du 17 Siècle par le S. Robert de Vougondy Geog. ord. du Roi du feu Roi de Pologne Duc de Lorraine et de Bar et de l'Academie royale des Sciences et Belles-lettres de Nanci, et Censeur royal*. Paris, 1772.

———. *Carte des Parties Nord et Ouest de l'Amerique dressee d'Apres les Relationes les plus Authentiques, 1764*. [Paris: Vaugondy, 1772].

[Vespucci, Juan]. "[Pesaro Map of the World, 1508]." Biblioteca e Musei Oliverana, Pesaro, Italy.

[———]. "[Planisphere, ca. 1520–1526]." Hispanic Society of America, New York.

————. *Totius orbis descriptio veterum quam recentium geographorum traditionaibus observata novum opus*. Florence, 1524.

von Reilly, Franz Johann Joseph. *Karte von Amerika*. [Vienna], 1795.

Waldseemüller, Martin. *Carta Marina Navigatoria Portugallen Navigationes Atque Tocius Cogniti Orbis*. Strassburg, 1516.

————. *Tabula Terra Nova*. Strassburg: Martin Waldseemüller, 1523.

————. *Universalis Cosmographia Secundum Ptholomaei Traditionen Et Americi Vespucii Aliorūque Lustrationes*. Strassburg: Martin Waldseemüller, 1507.

Werner, Johannes. [*Globe Projection-Graticule Diagram*]. In *Noua translatio primi libri geographiae Cl. Ptolomaei . . . & annotationas euisdem Ioannis Verneri*. Nuremberg, 1514.

Wytfliet, Cornelius. *Florida et Apalche*. Louvain, 1597.

————. *Hispania Nova*. In *Histoire vniverselle des Indes Occidentales et Orientales, et de la converion indiens*. Douay: Francisco Fabri, 1611.

"Xolotl." Códice Xolotl. Bibliothèque Nationale, Paris.

Zatta, Antonio. *America Settentrionale Divisa ne' Suoi principali Stati*. In *Atlante Novissi mo*. Venice: Zatta, [1775–85].

INDEX

Italicized page numbers followed by plate numbers indicate references to illustrations.